The FOSTER CARER'S Handbook

for carers of children 11 years and under (second edition)

by Ann Wheal

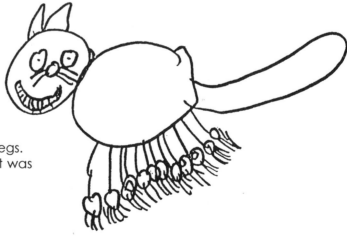

Brendan drew our cat. He was at the Willows Nursery School in Portsmouth. He drew the cat from one side. He went round the other side and could still see four legs so he drew four more. He then went to the front and could still see four legs. He finally gave up and decided the cat was having kittens.

Children have different ways of seeing

RHP

House Publishing

Russell House Publishing Limited

First Published in 1995 (Second Edition 2000) by

Russell House Publishing Limited
4 St George's House
Uplyme Road
Lyme Regis
Dorset
DT7 3LS
Tel: 01297 443948
Fax: 01297 442722
e-mail: help@russellhouse.co.uk

British Library Cataloguing-in-Publication Data:
A catalogue record of this book is available from the British Library

ISBN: 1-898924-86-4

Typeset by: The Hallamshire Press Limited, Sheffield

Printed by: Redwood Books, Trowbridge

Russell House Publishing

We are a group of practitioners and academics in social work,
probation, education and youth and community work who
collaborate with a professional publishing team. Our aim is to work
closely with the field to produce innovative and valuable material
to help managers, trainers, practitioners and students. We are keen
to receive feedback on publications and new ideas for future projects.

Contents

Section 8: Meetings   154

Section 9: Legal   166

Section 10: Other Information   176

Background

In 1992 the Department of Social Work Studies at the University of Southampton undertook a research project which became known as 'The Dolphin Project'.

During the project, the researchers met young people aged 11–18 who were being looked after in Birmingham, Berkshire and Hampshire. The young people talked about what they knew about the Children Act and also spoke about their time in children's homes and in foster care. The researchers also met the carers.

From the Dolphin Project, a report, called *Answering Back—A Young Person's View of the Children Act* was published by The Department of Social Work Studies, University of Southampton, Southampton, SO9 5NH.

The Foster Carer's Handbook is one of the many outcomes of this report.

For organisations wishing to combine this book with locally produced materials a loose leaf version is available (see insode back cover).

There is a similar book for 11–18 year old children entitled *Answers for Carers, You and the Young People In Your Care*, Ann Wheal, published by Pavilion Publishing Ltd.

This book seeks to discourage unfair discrimination on the grounds of age, gender, disability (including use of sign language), race, ethnic origin, nationality, sexuality, social class, religion or language.

NFCA welcomes this Handbook as a sound reference-base for foster carers. It is packed with useful information.

National Foster Care Association (NFCA)

Very informative. Something all foster carers should have.

Carer

I found this book easy to read and easy to refer to particular sections. Very thorough without being long winded. There are a lot of starting points for discussion with children as well as lots of practical information.

Carer

I think all social workers who work with children and foster carers, should be given this book and all foster carers, especially new carers. I thought the way you go through all the appropriate topics in a very simple to understand way was excellent.

Carer

I think it's brilliant. I use it all the time and I recommend it to other foster carers.

Carer

It's so easy to use and understand. It's the recommended book for those working on the NVQ course. I also use some of it with my own children.

Lecturer in Foster Care

Every parent should have this too!

Health Visitor

Acknowledgements

I would like to thank those who helped to create the first version of this book. Their contribution was invaluable.

I would like to thank those who have helped me during the production of the revised version:

Cathy Hill, Senior Lecturer in Community Child Health, University of Southampton
Cathy Caine, Policy Officer (Child Care), West Sussex County Council
Jan Hawkins, Foster Carer and Trainer
Simon Newstone, Foster Carer Resource Manager
Marion Layberry, Director, Independent Fostering Agency
Pam McCune, Co-ordinator Portsmouth Under Eights Forum and Mobile Crèche Service
    Manager, formerly Home Safety Inspector for Under 5s
Rachael McCune
Hilary Day, Parent Partnership Co-ordinator, Portsmouth
Jane Morgan, Educational Psychologist, Portsmouth City Council
Meriel Mann, Sandy Hookway and Gerry Emson, The Willows Special Educational Needs
    Nursery, Portsmouth
Ena Fry and Pat Verity, National Foster Care Association

I would also like to thank the following children for their super drawings:

Kate, Joe, Zach, Josef, Aaron, Jonathan, Leanne, Zoe, Louise, Cameron, Isobel, Laura, Yvette, Pippa, Megan, Daniel, Verity, James, Paul, Sallie, Catherine, Gavin, Andrew, James, Thomas, Joseph, Gemma, Cassey, Thomas, Rebecca, Emma, Edward and Sean as well as those children who forgot to put their names on their work. I would also like to thank many of the children from Bidbury School who helped in all sorts of ways.

As with all my books, I would also like to especially thank my husband Peter for his help, patience and guidance.

Foreword

Information is important for anyone to do their job. For foster carers it is vital that they have readily accessible information that they can call on whenever they need to. Information provides protection for carers. It helps them to understand their role and task, and the responsibilities that they and others have, but above all, it also helps to ensure protection for children.

Fostering is an isolated task. Foster carers, unlike their social work colleagues, are unlikely to be able to discuss issues with other people doing similar work on a daily basis. For many people in employment, their knowledge base grows through the normal everyday discussions, which go on in the workplace. Such a luxury isn't available to foster carers. However, a book, which brings together a wealth of knowledge on fostering issues, can become the information base that would normally be acquired by talking with others.

The previous edition of the Foster Carers Handbook proved invaluable, and gave carers throughout the UK basic information which laid the foundation for development, whether that was through training, or by fostering agencies providing additional written information. This book is a worthy successor, and has included within it even more topics; many of which have been suggested by carers and young people.

Pat Verity
Assistant Director, National Foster Care Association

Section 1: Introduction

Introduction

This handbook has been produced for foster and residential carers who are looking after children aged approximately 11 years and under.

Some of the aims of The Children Act 1989, The Children (Scotland) Act 1995 and the Children (Northern Ireland) Order are to:
- Encourage carers to work in partnership with children they are looking after and the children's families.
- Enable children to return to their families' homes as soon as possible if appropriate.
- Encourage carers looking after children to meet a broad range of children's needs and so help these children for the future.

It is not possible to learn to become a good carer by reading a book. The aim of this book is that it should be used as **a guide, referred to as necessary or dipped into when a particular topic arises**. It has been developed:
- For carers to read and use, and for carers to read and use with children, to help carers understand and to explain these matters to the children as appropriate.
- To help carers answer the many questions children under 11 years may ask about their time being looked after.
- To be used as a 'talking tool' when carers are working in partnership with children. In this way it is hoped the children, as they become adults, will learn to take responsibility for their own future.

The book contains many topics that may be used as a way to start talking with children about issues beyond the home.

Some people think that if a child is given too much information it may be misused. Our experience points to the reverse. The more information children have the better able they will be to plan successfully their lives and their future.

Everyone needs to be valued, to feel special, to feel important. By treating all children as individuals, working with and caring for them, a carer will build up their self esteem.
1. Most sections have at least one activity. Depending on the child's age and ability, the carer can either work through the activity with the child, or let them do it on their own and discuss the result afterwards if the child wishes.
2. The games, checklists, forms and pictures may be photocopied without permission.
3. All books and organisations mentioned throughout the text are detailed at the back of the book.

This book has been written so that it may be useful for:
- all carers of children of approximately 11 years and under
- anyone using the LAC (Looking after Children, Assessment and Action Records), child records produced by the Department of Health for use with looked after children
- those carers working towards NVQ and SNVQ qualifications
- people undertaking residential placements whilst studying for a social work qualification
- anyone working with children such as teachers, health visitors, school nurses, who wish to learn background information about looked after children and their carers

'A good carer is someone who sits down and listens to you and discusses things with you'

a young person's view

Note: *Some of the terms used in the book may vary from region to region; however the overriding principles are the same.*

National Standards in Foster Care

In 1999 the *National Standards in Foster Care* were published following extensive consultation with many interested parties including foster carers and young people.

The Report and Recommendations of the UK Joint Working Party on Foster Care and the *Code of Practice on the recruitment, assessment, approval, training, support and management of foster carers,* were published at the same time. Together, they charter the work of foster carers and the care of young people. The following is the summary of the standards published at the front of the document.

Section One of the *National Standards in Foster Care* covers the following topics designed to ensure the specific needs and rights of each child or young person in foster care are met and respected:

Equal opportunities and valuing diversity: *Children, young people and their families are provided with foster care services which value diversity and promote equality.*

Assessment of the needs of the child or young person: *An assessment of the child or young person's needs is made prior to any placement, communicated to all parties concerned and updated regularly.*

Care planning and reviews: *A written care plan is prepared for each child or young person placed in foster care; all aspects of the plan are implemented, it is reviewed regularly and any changes are made only as a result of a review meeting.*

Matching carers with children or young people: *Each child or young person placed in foster care is carefully matched with a carer capable of meeting their assessed needs.*

The child or young person's social worker: *Each child or young person placed in foster care has a designated social worker who ensures statutory requirements for their care and protection are met and promotes their welfare and development.*

A safe and positive environment: *The foster home provides a safe, healthy and nurturing environment for the child or young person.*

Safe caring: *Each child or young person in foster care is protected from all forms of abuse, neglect, exploitation and deprivation.*

Recording and access to information: *An up-to-date comprehensive case record is maintained for each child or young person in foster care which details the nature and quality of care provided, and contributes to an understanding of their life events. Relevant information from the case record should be made available to the child and to anyone involved in their care.*

Contact between children and their families and friends: *Each child or young person in foster care is encouraged to maintain and develop family contacts and friendships as set out in their care plan and or placement agreement.*

Health care and development: *Each child or young person in foster care receives health care which meets their needs for physical, emotional and social growth. They should also be given information and training appropriate to their age and understanding to enable informed participation in decisions about their health needs.*

Educational needs: *The learning and educational needs of each child or young person in foster care are given high priority and they are encouraged to attain their full potential.*

Preparation for adult life: *Each child or young person in foster care is helped to develop the skills, competence and knowledge necessary for adult living; they receive appropriate support and guidance for as long as necessary after being in foster care.*

Section Two seeks to ensure that effective and appropriate care is provided by each foster carer and covers:

Assessment and approval of foster carers: *Each foster carer is subject to, and participates in, a comprehensive assessment of their ability to carry out the fostering task. They must be formally approved by the appropriate authority before a child or young person is placed in their care.*

Supervision, support, information and advice for foster carers: *Each approved foster carer is supervised by a named, appropriately qualified social worker, and has access to adequate social work and other professional support, information and advice. This will enable them to provide consistent high quality care for each child or young person placed in their home.*

Training of foster carers: *Each foster carer is provided with the training necessary to equip them with the skills and knowledge to provide high quality care for each child or young person placed in their care.*

Annual reviews with carers: *A joint review is conducted with each carer at least once a year in a manner that:*
   a) *satisfies the authority of the continuing capacity of the carer to carry out the fostering task;*
   b) *provides the carer with an opportunity to give feedback;*
   c) *contributes to essential information on the quality and range of service provided by the authority; and*
   d) *forms recruitment, assessment and training strategies.*

Payment of allowances and expenses associated with caring for fostered children: *Each foster carer receives an allowance and agreed expenses which cover the full cost of caring for each child or young person placed with them.*

Section Three notes that each authority is responsible for the provision of public care for children and young people and the requirement to offer a high quality foster care service for all who could benefit from it by ensuring:

Effective policies: *Each authority has effective polices in place to promote and plan the provision of high quality foster care for children and young people who could benefit from it.*

Management structures: *Each authority has effective structures in place for the management and supervision of foster care services, staff and foster carers.*

Professional qualifications and appropriate training for social workers: *All social work staff responsible for the provision of fostering services are professionally qualified* *and appropriately trained to work with children and young people, their families and foster carers, and have a good understanding of foster care.*

Recruiting and retaining an appropriate range of carers: *Each authority ensures access to a supply of foster carers which meets the range of needs of the children and young people within its area.*

Reward payments to carers: *Each authority considers the implementation of a reward payment scheme for foster carers.*

The foster care panel: *Each authority convenes a fostering panel as part of its assessment and approval process for foster carers, which also plays a role in monitoring and developing local fostering policy, procedures and practice.*

Placement of children through other authorities or agencies: *An authority may contract out any aspect of the provision of foster care for a child or young person it is looking after with another authority or agency. When so doing, the authority responsible for the care of the child must ensure that legal requirements for their care are met and the care provided meets national quality standards and regulations for the foster care service.*

Representations and complaints procedures: *Children and young people, their parents, foster carers and other people involved are able to make effective representations, including complaints about any aspect of the fostering service, whether it is provided directly by an authority or by a contracted authority or agency.*

Section 2: The Carer

As a result of the publication of the national standards, the recruitment and retention of foster carers has undergone many changes. Some foster carers are now paid a wage instead of an allowance. Some are given formal job descriptions as paid employees. Those who are not should still be given a description of what is expected of them. The following is an example.

Sample job description

The purpose of foster caring is:
- To provide a safe, caring, healthy and nurturing environment.
- To help each child to recognise and overcome factors that have led to them being looked after, in order that they may achieve their potential.
- To assist with the preparation of each child for their future.

Key duties are:
- To help the child to develop their own basic physical care.
- To monitor and respond to the child's health needs.
- To help the child to develop self esteem through presentation and appearance, including an understanding of personal possessions.
- To support the child's education, including liaison with schools as appropriate.
- To develop the child's understanding and acceptance of routines, disciplines and structures.
- To develop the child's social behaviour and attitudes.
- To encourage the child to manage their own leisure time, ensuring opportunities for recreation and leisure activities.
- To assist with the child's religious development in keeping with their own and their family's cultural and religious beliefs.
- To promote an understanding of differences in race, culture, language and religion and a respect for those differences.
- To understand the legal requirements of foster caring.
- To hold a basic knowledge of first aid.
- To ensure that the child is kept safe from hazardous substances and ensure general safety in the home.
- To work with social workers and other agencies, as required including participation in multi-professional meetings about the child.
- To provide information, in writing or verbally, to social workers and other agencies, as required and to maintain a record of significant events.
- To ensure the best possible relations with the child's family, including working with agreed contact arrangements.
- To provide adequate insurance.
- To ensure good relations with the agency through efficient administration, and communication about a child's placement and regular attendance at training and meetings.
- To be involved in a mutual support network with other foster carers, as appropriate.
- To manage your own finances and tax affairs.
- To seek help immediately with any concerns relating to fostering.

Fostering panels

What are fostering panels?

Fostering panels are responsible for the assessment of applications to be foster carers, the approval and appointment of foster carers and the review and termination of foster placements.

Why do fostering panels exist?

In the interest of the child, the law demands that foster carers are competent and that foster carers and foster placements are monitored regularly. In the interests of foster carers it is important that the fostering process is accountable, and accessible.

Who makes up a fostering panel?

A fostering panel might be one person who can, without consultation, make decisions about approvals, assessments and terminations—although this is rare. Usually the panel comprises an assortment of people with appropriate experience and knowledge of the circumstances who can make informed decisions. Both systems have merit. There is no evidence that group decisions are necessarily better than an individual's decision—it depends on the people involved.

The important thing is that in arriving at any decision, account is taken of any relevant input about race, religion, culture, case history, medical history, legal implications etc. The Panel Chair should also ensure that the Panel contains some independent members. If, as the foster carer, you feel that there is someone who should be included, but has not been, you can appeal.

How does the fostering panel approve a foster carer?

When assessing an applicant to be a foster carer, the panel should ensure that:
- the criteria for approval are clear, documented and measurable, and that they are known to the applicant
- any reports or concerns about the applicant should be made known to the applicant in advance of any formal meeting
- any shortcomings that can be addressed by training or support are identified and made known to the applicant
- any decision arrived at is notified speedily to the applicant. Where the decision is to refuse an application, this should be done in person and the reasons given verbally and in writing.

Assessment and monitoring

In the interest of both the child and the foster carer all foster placements should be monitored. This is the responsibility of the fostering panel.

How is a 'placement' terminated?

If it is not in the interest of the child or the foster carer for the placement to continue then the Panel should take appropriate action. However they should ensure that:
- during the approval process clear measurable targets were set
- during the monitoring process, any unacceptable performance was explained and that targets and timescales for improvement were set
- appropriate (written) warnings were given and that adequate time was allowed for improvement to be made
- adequate support and training was given
- where neither the carer nor the fostered child is to blame for the termination, this is made clear. (This is especially important where a carer may wish to continue to foster.)

When a placement breaks down a disruption meeting should be held (see p 158).

Support for carers

Carers spend a good deal of their time either alone with the foster child or with their own family and the foster child. It is therefore vitally important that the carer is provided with a wide range of support to assist in the caring process. Foster carers must be valued by all staff with whom they come into contact.

Family placement workers (FPW) provide a link, and supervise and support the carer who should be given clear guidelines on the role of the FPW. They will represent the carer's views; ensure the placement quality standards are met; establish training needs and develop training plans for the carer, ensuring implementation. They will also work with the carer to develop a carer's career plan.

The child's social worker will provide full information about the child's background, history, family situation and reasons for placement as well as information on educational, medical, religious, linguistic, cultural and social needs. They may also give help and advice to the carer if a difficulty with the child arises.

Information for foster carers—Employers should provide foster carers with all the necessary procedures and practices including:

- the carer's role
- the law
- practice guidelines
- procedures if there is a complaint or allegation made against them (see p 12)

The annual review assesses the progress and work the carer has carried out during the previous year and sets goals for the future.

Training is an important source of support. In addition to basic training, carers will receive in-depth training on a variety of topics. It can be carried out in a range of ways, from individual one-to-one discussions through to full training courses (see p 14).

Access to specialist support may be particularly helpful for certain children. These might be psychiatrists, art, music or play therapists or counsellors.

Emergency support should be available 24-hours a day and the carer should have the procedures readily to hand.

Support groups can offer carers an opportunity to share experiences and learn from each other. They can offer peer support, friendship, empathy and mutual recognition.

Local foster care groups differ from support groups in important respects. They provide a forum for discussing wider policy issues that affect all carers. They can provide good support to carers who will meet other people who are not connected with them through any other means.

Agencies should provide a variety of support to local foster care groups. The group can provide valuable help in the development of the agency's policies, and a unique view of the service.

Types of foster care

There are three types of foster care, short, intermediate and long term. Briefly:

- Short-term placements are up to six months. Children with disabilities may receive planned short term placements at regular intervals for example.
- Intermediate placements are short-term placements that extend beyond the original period due to unforeseen circumstances.
- Long term placements occur when a permanent substitute family is provided for a child with the intention that the child is cared for outside their natural family for the rest of their life.

Within these three types, different sorts of foster care have devolved. The following pages have some examples.

Short-term programmed care, respite care, family link care and shared care

Some areas have several different schemes but the underlying principle is the same.

- Parents need a regular break from the child either so they can give their other children their attention or simply to have some time for themselves, to recharge their batteries.
- Children who have special needs or who require constant attention may be given respite care to allow the parents to have a break.
- Many parents of children who have special needs feel isolated as their child may not attend the local school or have friends locally. These types of care provide an opportunity for the child to meet other children and for the parents to get out and meet other people.
- A parent or another child in the family has gone into hospital, someone is very ill or there has been a death in the family.

These schemes may also be used because:

- there is a crisis in the family
- parents need time to sort out a problem
- the child needs a break from the parents

Schemes should be well planned and have the agreement of all parties.

Carers should:

- meet the child before the placement
- attend planning meetings
- be given all necessary information about diet, health, special needs, etc.

Outreach and family support

This work is not normally part of the carer's role but often they may be asked to look after or accommodate a child for a short period.

Much preventative work is being done nowadays with families who will be assigned a specially trained worker to help prevent the breakdown of a family. This worker may:

- give advice and guidance
- work with the family members individually or together
- take the child out maybe for the day, possibly on holiday
- set up day care for the child if they are not in school
- organise respite care for a short period

Support care

Support care is a caring alternative to traditional foster care. Support care offers:

- part-time foster care to children and their families on a time limited and contractual basis
- support to families and long term foster carers so they can continue to care for their child or young person
- local temporary placements for looked after children and young people placed in schools or residential units outside their home area

Support care recognises that:

- the stresses and strains of family life today can be too much and without some extra support, children and young people can end up being 'looked after' in public care
- some families are isolated—they don't have a grandparent, aunt, uncle or friend who can help out in a crisis
- leaving their family is very traumatic for children and can have repercussions throughout their life
- many children and young people do really well in foster care but sometimes the problems they bring with them will place a great strain on the foster family and 'extra' support can benefit everyone
- families in crisis may need a helping hand for a time but most will find their own long term solutions

Support carers offer care in many ways:

- at weekends (perhaps weekly, fortnightly or monthly)
- overnight stays during the week
- occasional 'time out' or a holiday away
- day care, for example, to cover school exclusion or in school holidays
- 'home leave' for young offenders preparing to come back to their home area
- retaining or building cultural links
- facilitating family contact where a child or young person is placed outside their original home area

Whilst agencies are committed to placing children and young people in homes that reflect their cultural and ethnic origin this is not always possible. Some dual heritage children and young people living with a white parent may also need to experience life in a family that reflects the other part of their dual heritage. Support carers from black or Asian origins offer a valuable opportunity to explore racial and cultural identity in a family setting.

Remand fostering

Remand fostering is for young people who having committed an offence who may benefit from living in a foster home rather than being placed in some form of secure accommodation. Whilst in a remand foster home the young person will work with the carer on ways to prevent re-offending. Remand foster carers receive additional specialised training to carry out this particular type of work.

Specialist fostering

In some locations specialist foster carers are being recruited and trained who have particular skills in dealing with especially difficult children. Emotional and behavioural difficulties may be indicated by a wide variety of forms including:

withdrawn	depressive or suicidal attitudes
disruptive	obsessive behaviour
anti-social or unco-operative behaviour	frustration, anger
pre-occupation with eating habits	threat of, or actual violence
school phobia	substance misuse

Men who foster

Men who foster can have an influential role in the lives of the children they look after. Many of these children will have previously experienced 'father' figures as absent, or abusive, and they may have confused expectations of a male foster carer. All carers, male and female, need to think about the role of male foster carers, and the positive impact that they can have on fostered children.

Most men who foster do so in partnership with a woman, but a minority do so as single male carers or in same sex relationships. Some men may be home-based and the main carer, while others may fulfil the more traditional role of family providers employed full-time outside the home. Whatever the working arrangements, men and women who foster are both responsible for the day-to-day care offered to children, and for communication with other professionals.

Research shows that fathers' involvement in children's lives can have a positive impact on their self-esteem, self-control, sociability, empathy and cognitive abilities. This involvement may take the form of substantial periods of time spent with children, in caring, play, helping with schoolwork, and sharing leisure activities. Sadly, more than half of fathers in the UK appear to spend less than five minutes a day one to one with their children.

Foster fathers' involvement has been seen to have a positive impact on the mental health of children, as well as contributing to greater placement stability. Men who foster offer a role model for young men and women. Foster fathers themselves identify some aspects of this 'positive male role model' as:

- a safe, caring, non-threatening male
- showing a range of feelings and emotions (not just anger)
- challenging stereotypes of men and women

Attention has been paid recently to the needs of boys for role models or mentors to help them work out their own sense of what being a man means for them. Research shows the importance of men highly involved in boys' lives (though this does not have to be a man resident in the household). Girls also need to see that men can be responsible and safe carers in particular.

Men who foster can be active in the following areas:

- joint decision making with his partner (if there is one) about fostering issues
- inclusion in all placement planning meetings
- spending time with social workers and other professionals
- attending training and other agency events
- spending individual time with fostered children
- taking an interest in children's education, health, and leisure activities
- giving thought to the role he is to play with each child including any safe caring issues

Safe caring

Many men who foster are concerned about safe caring advice and feel that their involvement with fostered children is severely limited by this advice. Men who foster have already undergone a thorough recruitment, assessment, and approval process, and should not be regarded as posing a safety risk to children. As long as social workers make efforts to meet with foster fathers, and to make training events accessible to them, then those men who try to evade contact with social workers will become obvious.

The main concern of foster fathers is the risk of false allegations against them, and how best to minimise this. A sensible, practical approach to safe caring issues will enable men to be involved carers, and to feel comfortable around children who have, or may have been abused.

Practical guidelines for all men who foster

- Understand the pattern of abuse a young person has previously suffered, and ask questions of the social worker—normal family routines can then be realistically adapted.
- Agree with the social worker how daily routines such as bedtimes and bath times should be approached based on the individual child's needs and allowing the foster father to give nurturing care.
- Offer positive one-to-one time with children—outings, leisure pursuits, help with homework, reading. Again, be clear with other professionals that this is ordinary family life and take advice on whether there are any particular risks attached.
- Offer children comfortable safe alternatives to sexualised behaviour. Don't avoid all intimacy—make it safe and ordinary for youngsters. As a family, allow and create opportunities to discuss sexuality, sexual abuse and emotions.
- Always keep a written record of significant incidents and signs. Be clear with the social worker what recording is required. Talk openly with your partner (if you have one), especially about your feelings and reactions to the fostered child. Let professionals know at the time if you are concerned about behaviour, not weeks afterwards.

The agency's role

Many men who foster feel isolated and unsure of their roles. Traditionally fostering has been regarded as an activity for women with men as supporters. This is changing, and many men are now 'lead carers' in fostering. They still often find themselves in the minority, as men, at meetings, and not in contact with other men who foster.

Agencies can do more to encourage and enable men to attend training courses, for example, running them at evenings or weekends, and offering some childcare support. They might offer more 'Men who Foster' events. Some men have commented that they thought they were on their own until they met with a group of other male foster carers.

Men who foster need to think about the responsibility they take for a child's education, health and social development and for engaging with the professional network around a child. The involvement of men as foster carers offers fostered children opportunities for improved development and for a different understanding of the role men can play in their lives. As one foster father said 'Helping to change a child's self esteem and ideas about himself, through offering a good male role model...'.

Allegations against carers

Some reasons why a child might make an allegation against a carer

- Something that has happened recently reminds the child of an event that took place before the child was with the carer.
- It is a way for the child to try to regain control over their life.
- The child sees it as a way of getting away from the home by making a false accusation.
- The child can misinterpret an innocent action, such as the carer putting an arm around them to offer comfort.

What can carers do to help prevent accusations being made against them?

- Keep a diary listing the main happenings for the day—it will be a very useful record in its own right regardless of the possibility of an accusation being made against you—and it could prove invaluable if you are wrongly accused.
- Introduce a safe rule—no-one touches another person's body without that person's permission.
- Help children learn to say NO if they don't want to be touched.
- Older children may need extra help to work out how to seek comfort from an adult without clinging to them.
- Avoid tickling and wrestling games.
- Ensure the child is always able to stay in physical control.
- Children who are old enough should bathe and wash themselves.
- Young children should be helped by carers of the same sex.
- Carers should not walk around in their underwear or night gowns.
- All children in the house should have dressing gowns and slippers and should wear them when walking around the house in their night-clothes.
- Carers should not share their bed with a child even if the child is ill.
- Provide children with a time of warmth and affection outside the bedroom, telling stories, reading, talking or having a hot drink together.
- Children should not share beds. If children share bedrooms, clear rules should apply.
- A child should travel in the back of a carer's car to avoid any suggestion of the child saying they were 'touched'.
- Children and especially young people may develop sexual feelings for their carers or members of the carer's family. The best way to avoid this situation is to openly discuss topics such as sex, feelings, emotions and relationships as they occur.

Unfortunately on some occasions, allegations against a particular carer, the sibling of the carer, another family member or friend may be true. All allegations must be reported and investigated.

If a complaint is made, an investigation must take place. Different local authorities will have different criteria for dealing with allegations of abuse but any complaint should be handled sensitively, carefully and swiftly.

Unfortunately in the haste to act on the allegations, the investigation is sometimes not handled well. These investigations are sometimes insensitive, heavy-handed and in secret causing even more stress and anxiety to the whole family.

> **You may be the last person know that an allegation has been made against you!**
> **In fact you may only find out when the police knock on your door!**
> **Start keeping records now—don't get caught out.**

What to do if you are accused of abuse

If an allegation is made carers should call the member of their family who is most likely to be able to help and contact their professional association and their local authority. Their own support groups should also be able to help. They will need advice from a solicitor with experience of dealing with abuse cases either via their professional association or independently. Unfortunately, carers are often 'assumed guilty until proven innocent'.

Independent fostering agencies

The term 'independent fostering agency' refers to those fostering agencies which operate independently of a local authority. They can be not-for-profit, voluntary organisations, or registered charities, or profit-making organisations. The number of independent fostering agencies in the UK is growing rapidly and they now account for a significant number of fostering placements.

The best of these provide a comprehensive, flexible and professional service to local authorities and to the children and young people placed with them. Some agencies specialise in particular areas of work, dealing, for example, with children in a certain age range or sibling groups, or with children having specific difficulties.

Independent agencies recruit, assess, train and carry out checks on prospective foster carers in the same way as local authorities. Many have an advisory or appointment panel, but legal approval of all foster placements can only be given by local authority panels. Children are referred by local authority social services departments, and therefore, each agency should be able to demonstrate that their policies and procedures are of an acceptable standard.

Most independent agencies provide comprehensive training for foster carers and acknowledge that they should be recognised as professionals. A high level of support is also offered by many of them, including access to professional back-up 24 hours a day.

The National Standards in Foster Care applies to both independent organisations and to local authorities. They form the basis for regulation and inspection governing foster care both in the independent and local authority sectors.

Foster carers who choose to work with independent agencies are usually self-employed.

A joint forum for independent agencies has been set up with the *National Foster Care Association* (NFCA). Its overall purposes are to promote the highest standards in foster care, to facilitate communication between the independent sector and local authorities, and to provide opportunities for exchanging ideas and information. Only those organisations that fulfil NFCA membership criteria and agree to abide by a code of conduct are invited to take part in the forum.

Insurance for carers

Foster carers take responsibility for finding out how their own insurance is affected by foster children and for getting information in writing of the cover or other arrangements in place by the fostering agency.

The Foster Placement (Children) Regulations 1991 require fostering agencies in England and Wales to enter into a Foster Care Agreement with each carer, setting out the terms and conditions of the fostering service. Included in this must be a statement of 'the agency's arrangements for meeting any legal liabilities of the foster carer arising by reason of placement'.

The arrangements must include how the agency will meet claims by or against foster carers in respect of damage, loss or injury, or legal defence costs. Options available to agencies include:

- A written indemnity to all foster carers stating that the authority accepts responsibility for damages and costs incurred as a direct consequence of fostering
- Extension of the authority's own insurance cover to include foster carers.

Checklist for insurance cover

Carers should be supplied with information, in writing, from the local authority or the director of the fostering agency about the insurance cover carried for:

- Malicious damage in the foster home caused by the foster child or their family.
- Theft from the foster home by the foster child or their family.
- Theft or damage caused by a foster child to other people's property.
- Legal expenses cover to provide legal advice to foster carers and court costs.
- Damage or personal injury to the foster child.
- Accidental damage by a foster child.

Carers should always keep their insurance company informed. Let them know in writing that you either propose to undertake fostering activities, or that you are continuing fostering. Ask the company to confirm in writing that for the purposes of the insurance policy, children you are looking after either as foster children, or on a respite care basis, are regarded as members of your family whilst they are with you.

NFCA membership provides insurance benefits for individual or family members. The limit is £50,000 for legal expenses should a member have a criminal case brought against them in the course of their fostering duty, providing they are not eligible for legal aid. There is no excess clause to this policy.

> **Remember insurance cover is only valid if you have it.**

Training and guidance for carers

Training plays a very important part in a carer's development. It begins with training to become a foster carer, and continues throughout the person's career on a wide variety of topics. It may lead to qualifications if the carer wishes or if it is the policy of the agency to have qualified carers, e.g. National Vocational Qualifications (NVQs or SNVQs in Scotland).

What are NVQs and SNVQs?

These are work-based qualifications where the skills and tasks carers do in their work are assessed whilst at work. Carers and the assessor, sometimes a colleague, negotiate what evidence of a particular task is needed and how and when it will be gathered. The assessor records the evidence which is then included in the portfolio of the carer. When there is evidence of competence in sufficient units, the carer may be awarded the relevant certificate.

There is no time limit to these awards. Many people take about two years but it can take a shorter time depending on experience and on the assessment arrangements. Work done in the past may also count towards the award. A unit cannot be failed. If the carer is found 'not yet competent' they can get more help and try again.

For further details contact NCVQ, 222 Euston Road, London, NW1 2BZ.

Note: *many colleges are also offering courses linked to NVQ.*

Some carers having achieved their NVQ move on to higher education and are studying for a variety of qualifications including academic degrees. Some universities, however, may not accept NVQs for undergraduate entry or may ask for additional evidence of achievement including the prospective student being asked to write a paper on a chosen subject.

Changes to the current NVQ should ensure that the qualification is sufficiently rigorous to prevent future applicants experiencing such difficulties.

Diploma in Social Work (DipSW)

This award is the professional qualification for all areas of social work, including work with children and young people. These programmes are becoming very flexible with more open and distance learning options and more part-time and modular routes available. There are additional opportunities for people to enter the DipSW course with the credits for the competencies they already have. There may be changes in this course in the future.

Postqualifying and advanced awards in social work

These are two awards for those who already have a Diploma in Social Work. Credits are gained towards the awards through work being assessed and approved. This can be done over a period of time. Work done in the past can also count towards these awards.

Other training opportunities

There are also many training courses available on subjects such as:

- counselling
- disability
- HIV/AIDS

- behaviour management
- family assistance
- first aid

- drug abuse
- law

The National Standards for Foster Care make it a requirement that joint training with family placement workers and social workers should take place. Involving young people in training is also an excellent idea.

Many people who have previously worked with children, young people and carers may find the change of culture, attitude and status of carers very difficult to accept. Everyone finds difficulty with change so some of the proposed changes may take longer to be implemented than it was intended. Training should help, particularly joint training.

Section 3: Being Looked After

Being looked after or being accommodated

When a child is first looked after by social services the child will probably have been under considerable stress. It is very important that this early stage is well planned and handled carefully. Each child will be different and will need to be treated differently. A child may want:

- to be on their own
- to talk to you alone
- to talk to someone else
- to very quickly become one of the 'gang'
- to talk to the carer's own children

Quite often a child may be rude or aggressive or even totally silent and not eat. Whatever their reaction in the first few days let them be alone—yet not alone—'be alert, watch and observe and be there when needed'. Other children can often help here.

Gradually try to persuade the child to take part in the life of their new home. Give them a welcoming, warm environment. Explain what is going on, why they are there, and if you know, how long the stay will be. Tell the child how the system works, who is responsible for them and who to go to if help is needed.

Give the child as much information as possible, at a pace they can take in and in language they can understand. It may be necessary to tell the child several times before they fully understand.

Let the child tell you about their previous experience, where they lived and what they say the rules were. Keep a note of what they say, it may be useful later. They could tell you about their previous schools, about people or pets who are important to them, in fact anything they want to tell you.

Social services should always plan a placement if at all possible. Then the parent and child can visit and meet the carers and talk about:

- what the child's normal routines, wants and worries are, including school and health concerns
- who lives in the home, the rules and routines. This gives everyone a chance to say if they think the child could be looked after there happily for the planned period
- visiting arrangements

In an emergency a child will be taken to a carer, often from a distressing situation. The child, social worker, parent and carer then have to catch up with the preparations. They must consider carefully what will help the child to settle in. Whether a carer better able to help that child can be found, perhaps nearer home or school.

Before a child is looked after there should have been a planning meeting and all the necessary arrangements made. The aim, in most cases, will be to get a child back living with their parents or guardians as soon as possible.

All local authorities will have different admissions procedures.

Working with parents

The various Children Acts state that contact between a child who is looked after and their family, and those connected with them must be encouraged. As far as possible carers should work in partnership with parents to encourage contact. Even if a care order is in force, contact must be allowed unless the order says otherwise.

Working with families is a particularly important part of a carer's role. It is crucial to make good links with a child's family within the first days or weeks of the child being looked after. This can determine how often a child will meet up with the family in the future and the likelihood of the child returning home.

The child's social worker should draw up a plan, as soon as possible, including contact with families and who will arrange the meetings. Local authorities may have different practices and carers should ensure the guidelines are followed. British Agencies for Adoption and Fostering (BAAF) have published a useful book *Contact: Managing Visits to Children Looked After Away from Home.*

How can carers help?

- Listen to what both sides have to say.
- Talk to the child regularly, about all sorts of things. A child will probably come round to talking about their family at some time.
- Listen if a child is talking to their teddy or their pet; they *may* be acting out a reality but don't jump to conclusions.
- Find out all the facts.
- Take things slowly, one step at a time. Don't rush.
- Talk to other people who may know the child so you can learn as much as possible about the child, such as their culture or religion.

Sometimes a brother, sister, grandparent, relative or friend can act as a go-between. If a first meeting is arranged, carers should talk over with the parent where it should be. It could be on neutral ground such as a McDonalds, or Pizza Hut or carers could invite the parent to the home if the child agrees. If either party refuses to make contact at first, don't give up, be sensitive to the difficulties.

There will probably be lots of hate or hurt: explain things as you see them to both sides. There may also be feelings of guilt—children often mistakenly think 'it's my fault'. Most children really do want contact with parents even if they won't admit it.

There are practical things that could be done to encourage keeping contact with families:
- Don't rush into getting the child to make contact too soon; the child may not be ready. Children may appear upset but may really want to see their parents. A letter or telephone call telling them the news may be a good idea in the first place.
- Talk to the parents about the child; tell them the good things.
- Encourage the parents to see the child.
- Be honest; talk plainly; use suitable language.
- Don't make judgements; find out the facts.
- Try to get communication going, at first by you leading the talking.

Sometimes the foster carer is the 'piggy in the middle' with the child playing the parent off against the carer and vice versa. Areas of conflict between the two might be:
- clothes
- diet
- manners
- bedtimes
- sweets
- speech
- video games
- food
- hairstyles
- TV
- money

The child may go home for a visit and return in a very awkward or aggressive frame of mind. Carers need to understand and respect the different values a family might have. It may also be a way of the child showing their confusion or unhappiness. Usually this challenging behaviour won't last very long especially if there are plenty of interesting things planned.

If the child is going to meet the family, you may have to explain why they are going, how long they will be there and where the meeting will take place.

The child's family may have very different rituals or ways of celebrating them. Find out what they are if possible (p 45 may help).

Above all foster carers must respect the child's family, as in most cases the child will eventually live back with their parents.

The following are some examples carers told us are sometimes useful for working with parents:

Example 1

Visits from parents can be difficult. If it is possible, parents could do 'normal' things such as preparing food, feeding the child, washing up, bathing, walking to the park. Talking about what the child is doing is another way of getting conversation going. This might be:
- the child arranging bricks, boxes, toys, in fact anything and saying what is being made
- drawing, painting or modelling—beware of parents who want to show the child how to do it or to improve the child's picture

Example 2

The parents might like to draw a picture, they could talk about it with the child. It also gives the parent something to do whilst they are talking.

Give both the parents and the child a large sheet of paper on which a straight line has been drawn across the middle of the page. This line should be marked with different periods of the child's life, if the child is seven, say, divide the line into seven sections.

Ask the child and the parents to separately draw the good points they remember about their life above the line and the bad points below the line. A young child may need your help—they could put a mark and tell you about it. You could draw it for them or make a note for later.

Parents are invariably amazed at the difference in responses between what they thought and what the child thought. Often common ground is found for talking together about the things they had both enjoyed. It may also give some clues on matters that need resolving.

Example 3

A similar idea is to get the child to draw a picture of a wiggley road or pathway. Explain to the child that this road is their life and ask them to mark the good times and the bad times on the wiggley road. The 'ups' on the road are good times and the 'downs' the bad or not so good times. If they wish the child could draw 2 roads. The child and parent could write on one road each. The carer could help the child if necessary.

Example 4

Carers could perhaps organise an outing, maybe to the park or a picnic or take them all out for a car ride and then chat about it afterwards over tea.

One point to remember is that sometimes parents are not, or think they are not, good at writing and spelling. Very tactful help may be needed if a parent is asked to write anything.

Once you have got the contact going, you will have to help to keep it going. You will probably also have to explain to both parties:

- just what 'working in partnership' means in practice
- what the benefits are for both sides
- that talking and discussing are better than arguing and shouting

However, if it really won't work out, have a plan ready so you know how you will handle the situation from both sides. Of course there will be set backs, these are only to be expected.

Act as a mediator if you can by:

- encouraging the contact
- keeping the contact going
- telling the family all the positive news about the child
- ensuring it is possible for the child to meet their parents in private if they wish or if it is appropriate
- giving the parents an explanation if their child shows anger towards them or appears disloyal because he or she turns to you for comfort
- sensitively correcting the child if they call you 'Mum' or 'Dad' and discussing this openly with the child's mother or father

- asking the parents about specific cultural or religious matters if you need advice
- respecting parents wishes about which school or playgroup they would prefer the child to attend if at all possible and discussing all such related matters with them
- helping the child to remember family birthdays and other important times
- inviting families to special events
- taking a video film of particular events in a child's life such as sports day or school play
- encouraging telephone contact and letters
- encouraging the exchange of photographs
- being welcoming when families come
- telling parents that their travelling expenses may be paid by the social services department
- sharing information

There may be other important people in a child's life such as grandparents, friends and teachers. The child may need help to keep in touch with these people.

Caring for children
General considerations

'*Fostering is fun; fostering is hard work. Fostering requires patience and tolerance*' said a foster carer member of our working party. This statement is true of all caring.

Most children under 11 who are looked after will be fostered. Social services will try to find a carer who:
- has the same background and racial origin
- has the same religion (if they have one)
- understands the child's needs
- speaks the same language if at all possible

Carers are encouraged to work with parents unless there is a court order stating otherwise.

Some things for carers to think about when a child arrives.

The home the carer is providing may be quite different from that which the child is used to such as:
- the house may be heated in a different way
- there is different bedding
- clothes are expected to be folded or put away on hangers
- everyone wears slippers or shoes in the home
- eating habits are different and there are set mealtime rules in the house
- some people use a cup and saucer, not a mug
- talking with mouth full is or isn't accepted
- interrupting when someone is speaking is or is not allowed
- what the child should call the carer
- what the carer tells the child about, e.g. the carer's own personal information
- there may be a man in the home. Many children from single parent households may find this strange
- do you have to ask or wait to be invited to help yourself to, say, a biscuit. Can you only take one or three or four?

Things disabled children can usually do for themselves may not now be possible. Physical aids for example may not be in the house or practical arrangements have not been set up.

Practical things that might be different when the child walks through the door of the home:

- size of house
- furniture
- curtains
- carpets
- toilet paper
- food and where it is kept
- garden
- pets or no pets
- beds and bedding
- toothbrush and paste
- fluffy towels
- alcohol on display
- toys
- language and communication
- relaxed or formal atmosphere

Practical differences a disabled child might notice include less or more space for equipment. To help a child settle, the foster carer may need to learn details of how a child likes to be fed, changed, and the routines, especially for a child with limited communication.

A child will notice some of these differences and may be puzzled. They might also cause silent worries.

Some ideas to help children cope with the differences without changing or losing their own identity:

- What was their lunch box like? Would they like a similar one, or a different one?
- Did Mum or their previous carer walk them to school or did they go on their own?
- Are they used to helping around the house? Would they like to help?
- Did they get any pocket money?
- Do they like pets including the carer's pets? Did they have a pet?
- Were they used to noisy play, did they go to play at friends' homes?
- Has the child got a comforter and what is it called. Smells are particularly important to children and they usually hate their comforter or soft toys to be washed. Older children may have a comforter but may be embarrassed about anyone knowing.
- If the child is old enough, let them help you choose what they wear and to select new clothes with your help. Don't throw away children's clothes that they bring with them. Use them if possible, especially in the early days or if the child wants to wear them.
- Don't cut the child's hair or change their appearance without discussing this with the parents and getting their consent. Sikh boys are not supposed to have their hair cut. They may want to have their hair cut but their parents may not want this.
- A child may be uncomfortable bathing or undressing in front of a stranger - be sensitive and find out what they are used to.
- Get them to go to the same school if at all possible, even if social services need to provide transport.

When the child arrives:

- Start the way you mean to go on—in other words don't shower the child with gifts or let them behave in a particular way if you're going to change the rules later.
- Be understanding.
- Accept them for what they are.
- Be super-aware.
- Make sure you have checked the list given to you by the social worker telling you about the child. Ask if you need more information, such as about a comforter and favourite toys; what the child calls using the toilet; food—likes, dislikes, allergies; health problems, bedtime routine, e.g. sleeping alone, light out or on.
  Is there anything else the carers should be told that might be relevant? Check the information with the child, the parent and the social worker.

- Tell the other children about the new child—keep them involved.
- Have a welcoming tea where everyone can meet each other.
- Don't treat one child better than another. All children's needs are different.
- Remember the child has parents; don't deny them to the child even if you think they are awful!
- If you know them, continue with the routines, such as bedtimes, the child is used to, and use similar words and language.
- Try to find out what the child wants to know? Their questions may be sideways on, e.g. what happened to 'Edward' when his mother came out of hospital? Explain all you can, maybe run through once, maybe in small bursts.
- 'Normalise'—remind the child of similar things that have happened to others, then they won't feel too different. For example if their mother used a childminder it didn't mean the child was not loved!
- Find ways to reassure the child and talk about what the child can do to help things get back to normal quickly, like telephoning family or seeing friends.
- If the child is naughty, don't say 'Your Mum wouldn't like it'. What caused the naughtiness—look at patterns such as time of day, bed times, did something trigger bad memories?

The child will want to fit in and be the same with their carer but will be confused when they have contact with their own family and the carer's family. When the child feels confused they may:

answer back   **kick out**   **go quiet**

What the child thinks and feels is very important.

Being looked after is always about a temporary situation which should have been explained to the child. It may cause them to feel they don't belong anywhere. Six weeks in a child's life may seem like eternity to them.

If the child is old enough to understand:
- explain what a social worker does
- what their court order means if they have one
- what the many new terms they will hear mean
- what the role of a carer is

Be honest with the child.

The child will need help to make sense of what is happening. Don't be put off if you are rejected at first. Try again. Try a different approach. Gradually they'll come round and want to talk. Social services have a responsibility to provide trained interpreters if required.

What else can carers do?

- Attend all the meetings about the child (social services can make child care provision to help you do this).
- Give observations of the child.
- Speak on behalf of the child at meetings if the child wishes—it is often easier for the child to tell someone they are relaxed with rather than their social worker or their parent, or for them to speak at a meeting.
- It may help to write down what the child says. It will act as a reminder and it will give the child confidence if they see and agree what has been written.
- If asked the carer may attend court to give evidence.
- Carers should keep a diary and record the events of each day.

If things are really difficult and the carer feels unable to have the child's family visit the home, alternative arrangements can be made by the social worker. It is important that the carer is honest about the way they feel and why.

Living with relatives

Sometimes when a child cannot live at home they may go to live with relatives or friends such as grandparents who may become foster carers; sometimes this is known as network care or kinship care or friends and family who are carers (FFAC).

In many cases this is ideal as the child will be living with people they know; the customs and traditions will be similar and contact with parents may be easier; they will be able to go to the same school and clubs and keep the same friends.

On the other hand some children who are looked after by grandparents feel that there is not enough independence. A child may feel the grandparents are always on the side of the parents. They may also blame the grandparents for what has happened.

Fostering

Being fostered, what does it mean?

It means a child (and hopefully any brothers and sisters) will be looked after by a person, called a foster carer, in the carer's own home. This may be either for a short time while things are sorted out at home or for a longer period, depending on the situation.

Can anyone be a foster carer?

No. Anyone can apply but carers are carefully chosen. Social services will try to find for a child a foster carer who:

- has the same race, language, culture and social class
- has the same religion (if they have one)
- understands the child's needs

Living with a family

Most children will live with a family of some kind.

Living with a family will have different meanings to different people. It may mean:
- a couple living alone
- a couple and child
- an extended family such as grandparents, uncles or aunts
- a single parent possibly with visiting partner
- one parent and a step parent plus parents' child
- one parent and a step parent plus both parents' children
- two parents' children plus foster children
- a household with pets
- no pets when the child is used to pets

No two families are the same. There will be differences in:
- customs and traditions
- values
- atmosphere—formal or informal
- expectations
- attitudes to noise, shouting, play
- religion
- acceptable standards of behaviour

When a child is first fostered, the culture shock may be tremendous. If the fostering is planned then the gradual build-up of visits will make the transition easier.

Wherever possible black children should be fostered with families from similar ethnic backgrounds. The placement should take into account the specific linguistic, cultural, physical, emotional and religious needs of the child.

Children who have not been used to close family relationships often find living in such a family hard to handle.

Before any child is fostered it is extremely important that a written agreement is drawn up and signed. Even at the risk of being seen as awkward or fussy by social services, foster carers should ensure that they 'dot every i and cross every t'.

In other words find out:
- what is known about the child, the child's family and friends
- who decides what issues need to be decided, and by whom
- what parental contact there will be, when and how
- what other relevant information is known
- what is expected from the placement
- what support, if any, will be given
- if things go wrong, what is the procedure

The written agreement must be realistic.

What financial help do foster carers get?
- The agency must pay foster carers an appropriate allowance or salary which ensures the foster carer will not be out of pocket as a result of the service they are providing.
- All the details should be clearly written in the agreement and understood by the carer.

What should the carer call the child?
- Let the child choose but it is best to encourage a child to use their own name to preserve their sense of identity with the family.
- Children cannot change their surname. If they want to use the name of the family they are living with they may need help with spelling and practice in writing it. Wherever possible children should keep their family surname.
- The child may have a family name or a nickname. This may be personal and they may not want anyone else to use it.

Whilst the child is with you

- Be open and honest.
- A child may not be used to a routine so may take time to adjust.
- Look for the positives.
- Foster carer's own children often tell the child the home rules before the carer has decided the time is right.
- If the child is of school age get them back to school as soon as you feel the child is ready, preferably to the school they are used to. However, if the stay is long term sometimes the child may want to attend the same school as the rest of the family. You may have to seek advice from the child's parent, social worker and the schools about this and about the best time to change schools.
- Don't rush to become the child's friend, but wait and gradually build up the relationship. With a 'frozen' child this may take ages. The child may need specialist help. On the other hand some children will be waiting for some encouragement from the carer.
- There may be routine things everyone does as a family such as clearing the table, washing the dishes, cleaning their room etc. Encourage the child to join in.

- Foster families need to be sure that no-one leaves themselves open to accusations, or misunderstandings, or behaves in a way a child might find threatening or remind them of things in their past (see p 11).
- Value any possessions a child may bring with them.
- If the child brings their drawings or paintings back from play group or school give them a place where the pictures can be put on display.
- Help the child in every way possible to develop and grow so they will be able to take their place in society.

Children with special needs or a disability

Children with special needs may have problems such as:

- health
- social
- emotional
- physical movement
- learning
- communication

Some children may have a combination of problems, such as a physical disability and problems with communication; or cerebral palsy and visual impairment. This will compound the child's difficulties and also make caring for the child more difficult.

Whatever the child's problem is, the carer needs to find out as much information about the child from all quarters, if possible, before the placement so they will be able to help the child. This may mean asking the:

- social worker
- parents
- teacher
- health visitor
- specialist nurse if the child is say a diabetic
- doctor
- other specialists such as a speech therapist

Quite often a child with special needs has become too difficult for the parents to cope with and that is the reason they are being looked after. Behavioural problems can occur which may be a sign of frustration or the only way that the child has been able to get attention.

How can carers help?

- Obtain as much knowledge regarding the special needs or disability as possible.
- Have high but realistic, expectations of the child.
- Stress the good things a child can do.
- Praise the child, reassure them.
- Encourage the child to take part in a wide variety of activities.
- Help or teach them to play.
- Help the child to mix with others.
- Help them become as independent as possible.
- Don't treat them differently.
- Talk to them, discuss, explain.
- Sometimes children with special needs need firm boundaries—so set them.
- Be patient.
- Social skills may also need to be taught, such as eating, drinking, using the toilet.

Sometimes children with special needs don't sleep well at night so it is essential that they go to bed tired and ready for sleep. During the day:

- keep them lively
- keep their brain working and stretched
- keep them busy

They could do jobs if they are able, such as lay the table, pick up things like newspapers or tins in the supermarket for you; in fact anything that will keep them physically and mentally active. Too often they are allowed to vegetate. If the child needs special equipment or the home needs to be adapted, carers should discuss this with the social worker and decide what changes are appropriate.

> **Caring for children with special needs can be very time consuming and wearing but it can also be extremely rewarding.**

Siblings and family groups

There are really two different yet similar groups here—the foster carer's own children and the group of children who come as a family to be fostered. Both may have:

- group loyalty which may not always seem logical
- an emotional bond
- group support
- a leader, not always the oldest
- group identity

It is particularly important that both groups retain their identity. Later on the group may use the other's members as scapegoats in a disagreement!

Sometimes siblings are not fostered together. If appropriate, carers should encourage contact to be maintained or developed.

Foster children

If several children from one family are fostered they will often stick very closely together and behave in a particular way. It may be that one out of, say, four children will refuse to go to bed, so they all refuse. Meal times may be another cause for conflict.

It is important to respect this group loyalty, not to undermine it. As the children become more secure in their new home they will gradually come round—don't rush but help them to become individuals whilst still retaining their family loyalties.

The children of foster carers

It is always essential to have the commitment of the whole family as a unit. Both sides must always be honest with each other.

Honesty about:

- what the future will be like; some things will have to change
- what to expect of the foster child
- what everyone thinks and feels
- what problems there might be, in the home, at school etc.

> ## Example 1
>
> Brian, a foster carer, said that when he and his wife decided to foster they thought they had looked at the decision from every angle and explained things to their children. However, they had forgotten about certain family traditions one of which was that Sunday morning was a family time. Their children all came into and onto the bed with them when they had hot coffee and bread rolls together as a family.
>
> On the first Sunday after Sandie, their teenage foster child arrived, it suddenly dawned on the whole family that their Sunday breakfast would never be the same again.
>
> There are two problems that needed sorting here, one was the unplanned and un-expected outcome of fostering the child and secondly the intrusion into the family privacy.

Many people still regard foster children as problem children. They have fixed ideas. There is still a stigma. Children of foster carers need to be given:
- facts and information about fostering
- a few stock answers to awkward questions—'don't be nosy' might be what they want to say but daren't!

Foster carer's children also need to know that:
- they have rights as members of a family
- they will be listened to
- that the carer will be open and frank with them
- that they should be open and frank with their parents

> ## Example 2
>
> Kate, a carer, told us that her son asked 'When is it my turn to move out?'. She thought she had explained everything to James but obviously she had failed.

Carers and their children could perhaps draw up an informal contract with agreed rules for all on:
- acceptable language
- meals and meal times
- bed times
- coming-in times
- pocket money
- home rules, such as if a child gets up in the night, should they flush the toilet

Don't impose these on the foster child straight away.

Some other areas of possible conflict:
- The foster carer's children think that the social worker spoils the foster child, e.g. takes the child to McDonalds. The foster carer's children don't go, yet when there is a family outing, everyone goes.
- The foster child is not used to regular, interesting meals, and will only eat sausage and chips. The carer gives the child sausage and chips to help the settling in process so the foster carer's child wants sausage and chips too.
- The foster carer seems to spend more time with the foster child. No matter how exhausted the carer is they should try to spend some time each day with their own children as well as with the foster child—everyone needs to feel an 'only child' at some time.
- The foster child sees the foster carer's children with better things than they have and vice versa.

In some regions, groups have been set up for the children of foster carers. Some independent foster agencies seem particularly good at involving these children in the fostering process and local authorities should learn from this practice. More needs to be done to ensure the voice of the children of foster carers is heard.

Problems should not be allowed to stew.
Now is the best time to talk if there is a problem or worry.

Missing out on childhood

Both foster children and foster carer's children may miss out on childhood in some ways.

Foster carer's children often:
- take on the responsibility for the new children
- have children coming to live with them and just when they know them the foster child moves on
- may see conflicting behaviour that would not be acceptable to them or by them to their parents
- have many visitors coming and going to their home
- may feel the resentment of friends and family

Foster children **may have:**
- had the responsibility of helping run the home or looking after the family for a long time
- been abused and may need help and counselling.
- been picked on or bullied because of their size or their clothes and become protective towards their brothers and sisters
- moved on several times with different families

Example

Cathy's foster child, Dan aged seven, recently upset his teacher by challenging her behaviour. The teacher was talking to Dan in a particular way. Dan said 'I don't think you are being fair'. The teacher's response was 'How dare you say what is fair?'. At home, being treated fairly was something that was discussed openly and if anyone felt something was not 'fair', Cathy would stop, consider the situation and talk about it with the family.

Cathy discussed the matter with the teacher concerned and the head teacher, in case similar situations arose in the future.

Bullying may occur between children who are fostered and the carer's own children, and possibly vice versa. Carers need to keep a close watch on this and have a strategy ready should it occur.

Children's homes

Children's homes are run by people who really want to look after children who cannot be looked after in a family. All children's homes that are not maintained by the local authority have to be registered by social services or the Department of Health.

Some very small homes which are unregistered have to be visited by social workers to make sure the staff look after the children properly.

Children's homes try to provide children who cannot live at home with the best possible quality of life in the circumstances. Children under ten are usually only accommodated in children's homes when it enables them to live with older brothers and sisters, or, in exceptional circumstances, until a suitable foster carer can be found.

Occasionally the home will be separated into sections so that children live in groups of 6–10 children. They will share some facilities such as dining room, TV room with the other children living there. If there is education on the premises, they may share teachers. They will also spend some of their time with the other children in the home.

A keyworker will be made responsible for a particular child. This keyworker will welcome the child to the home making them feel important and talk over successes and worries. The keyworker will also:
- help the child to keep in contact with family and friends
- encourage the child at school and support the child by contact with teachers, attending open evenings, etc.
- take a special interest in the child, and attend meetings to promote the child's interests
- listen and encourage the child to talk over any worries
- encourage the child to take part in hobbies and clubs, and to make and keep friends

In all homes, there will always be someone who has overall responsibility. All the staff work a shift system, which means there will always be someone available 24 hours a day, 365 days a year.

If a child has a problem or wishes to make a complaint, the child should tell their key worker, the home manager or their social worker. Everyone should be aware of the complaints procedure for their home.

The home environment

The best children's home I ever visited had been the family house of the home manager and her husband, who had converted it to a children's home. It felt like a home. It looked like home. It was home to all the residents, and as such was respected by them.

The environment in which we all live is really important, much more important than many realise. A young person said that although the staff seemed nicer at a particular home, she wouldn't go there because 'It was a mess. How could I take my friends to a place like that?'.

It is important to involve children in how the home is organised, whether in a foster home or children's home, as this will help them establish an identity, a sense of belonging.

What should a child's room be like?

- Ideally, children should have their own room, though some children prefer sharing rooms. If it is not possible for them to have their own room, then they should have their own space in an agreed part of a room where they can put up pictures, posters, etc. Gradually give them responsibility for keeping the room or their space clean and tidy.
- If they are sharing, let them agree the ground rules with the other occupant.
- Carers should respect privacy. As they get older the child can help with cleaning their room and certainly keeping it tidy. In this way carers will not need to go into an older child's room unless the child is there.

Around the house, things that may seem unimportant at the time may have more of an impact than you think.

- If something gets broken or damaged, don't just leave it or call in the expert to do the job. If possible, work with the child who caused the damage in helping to put it right. They'll respect it more next time.
- A few indoor plants here and there will give a good feeling to a home particularly if grown by the child, and certainly nurtured by them. If possible, give the child a small plot of garden and help them to grow plants there. Not only will they be learning life skills but the child will get the satisfaction from a job well done and be able to admire the results of their efforts.
- If food is set out with care it seems to taste much better.

If everyone sets standards, children will remember them in the future.

It would be helpful if the kitchen, for example, reflected the child's culture and religion such as having spices, yams, lentils or other pulses around. Books, both for adults and children, about multi-cultural Britain would also be helpful.

It is all part of building up confidence, making them feel important and making them feel they are taking part in decisions, no matter how small, that affect their lives.

Collecting mementoes

Talking about their past is often a very painful experience for children and many don't want to do it. Others will be extremely keen to learn as much as they can.

All children who are looked after will have a past, a present and a future. Wait until you feel the time is right to talk to the child about where they have lived, who they have lived with, what memories they have and what more they would like to know.

Collecting mementoes is a way of filling in the jigsaw of a child's life, both in the past and for the future. When a child is older they will know things about themselves which they will be able to share with their own family and friends.

They may bring with them mementoes that are important to them, or they may, out of choice, bring nothing, hoping to wipe out bitter memories. On the other hand they may have nothing to bring.

What is a treasure to one child may be trash to another. Children should decide what they want to bring.

Respecting personal possessions may be a hard lesson for some children to learn, but one worth learning. Everyone will be different and all your skill will be needed in this area.

Carers could keep an envelope handy for the children where you or they can pop in mementoes or photos and keep them safe, or a trunk could be decorated by the child and used as a memento box.

It's also worth keeping a good filing system of negatives and photographs taken, as it can be disappointing for the child when they decide they want to remember a particular event, and the negatives can't be found!

> **It is important that children leave their placement with positive memories.**

Many children will do some Life Work (sometimes known as Life Story Work) so the following gives some more details.

Life work

Life Work (or Life Story Work) is a way of giving children a chance to learn about their past life and history. It should help them to understand some of the things that have happened. Often the information is put together safely into an album which may be called a Life Book. This work should be sensitively and carefully done by a specialist who may be a social worker. There is a book entitled 'Life Story Work' which is published by BAAF.

Black children may also need help to understand about immigration patterns and why their family is in a minority.

But I know all about me!

You might think you do but often your memory, or what you have been told, is not correct. Will you remember when you are an adult? Who will be around to tell you?

Some information will be on a social services file but things like photographs and keepsakes need to be put together whilst they can still be found. Sadly though, information sometimes just cannot be found.

How long will it take to do?

That depends on whoever is doing life story work with the child—but it might be once a week for, say, an hour or two. It depends on whether they will be going out to take photographs and make visits or whether it is just a question of organising what is already there.

Some ideas might be:
- drawing family trees
- tracing maps
- putting photographs into an album
- writing down memories after a chat
- visiting cemeteries to look at gravestones

It all depends on how much the child wants to include or how much research they want to do.

Must everyone do it?

Everyone has a right to privacy so of course the answer is 'No'. Sometimes adults are keener for Life Work to be done than the children themselves. Children should not be pressurised into doing it. Often children who have left 'care' say they wish they had done it.

Whose book is it?

It belongs to the child but you may offer to keep it in a safe place as photographs and keepsakes cannot be replaced. But it really is up to the child what they do with it and to whom they show it.

It is also a good idea to add to it with photographs and mementoes of the child's time being looked after.

Adoption

There are over half a million adopted people living in Britain today. The present government are looking into the possibility of making changes to the adoption law particularly with the view to speeding up the adoption process. However, the over-riding principles will remain the same.

To adopt—what does it mean? The dictionary says 'to take voluntarily as one's own child'.

Adoption is a legal term and since an adoption order is made by the court it cannot be changed. Adoption is something that affects all those involved throughout their lives: children, adoptive parents, birth parents and the families of everyone.

What is an adoptive family?

An adoptive family is a family who want to let a child become permanent members of their family, *legally, physically, socially* and *emotionally*.

In other words the child will live with their adoptive parents and be cared for as their own children whilst acknowledging they still have a birth family.

When do children get adopted?

Babies—some babies are placed with approved families who would like to adopt them shortly after birth. Others will be placed with foster carers until plans are clearer as to what is best for the child. This time will be as short as possible so that the baby can be returned to the birth family if that is possible or placed with a permanent family with a view to adoption.

Children—a child may be adopted when their birth parents cannot give them the care they need throughout their childhood or, occasionally, when the child's birth parents have died. The time taken before a child is formally adopted will vary according to circumstances. However a considerable number of checks must always be made to ensure adoption is right for the child.

How do I know how being adopted will affect the child?

When it is decided that a child can no longer live at home, a plan is drawn up. All the possible options are thought about and one of the possibilities may be adoption. Everyone involved is asked what they think, including the birth family wherever possible. The carers will also be asked what they think.

The child's social worker or carer will explain everything to the child. Provided a child is old enough to understand then their wishes and feelings must be considered.

Finding the right family

Many people—couples or single people with or without children already—apply to become adoptive parents. Thorough checks and interviews take place and a report goes to the adoption panel before a family can be approved and placed on a list of people who wish to adopt. They then wait until the right child is found.

To ensure that the child's needs are fully met, social services will try to choose a family who will have similar race, religion, language and culture to the child. Often brothers and sisters need to be kept together and so a family will be sought who can take all the sibling group.

Social services will also choose the type of family with whom the child can feel most comfortable and who are understanding and accepting of their past experiences and family backgrounds.

Occasionally the foster family with whom the child is living would like to adopt the child. If this is the case the foster family will have to be assessed for adoption. The checks and medicals will be different from the checks made when someone wishes to foster as there are differing implications.

In certain cases, local authorities can help families who want to adopt but are unable to because they are on a low income.

What does a family who want to adopt need?

- energy
- stamina
- patience
- understanding
- sense of humour
- flexibility
- realistic expectations
- firmness
- an ability and willingness to seek help when necessary

They will also need to see the potential of the child, to be able to help the child overcome their problems or difficult past experiences, and to always have the child's well-being at heart including the child's need for contact after adoption if this is appropriate.

What is an adoption panel?

It is a group of between 5–10 people which includes someone from social services and may include others who are teachers, health visitors or members of a voluntary agency, who meet to make sure:
- the adoption is in the child's best interest
- the family is suitable to adopt
- the child and family are the right 'match' for each other

If a child is going to be adopted, what happens?

1. The child and the adoptive family meet, usually in the child's existing home, to see if they like each other.
2. They usually meet several times again, and the family may take the child for an outing.
3. The child will begin to visit the adoptive family's home.
4. Several forms will be completed, progress discussed with everyone involved, and if everyone is happy, especially the child, a date will be agreed for the child to begin living with the adopters.
5. Later, when the child and the new family feel ready, an application will be made to the court for an adoption hearing, and a report on the adoption will be given to the court.
6. Other people will become involved (see p 161).

Before the child can be adopted the mother, and usually the father, will have been asked to sign a form to give their permission for the adoption. They will also be asked what sort of family they would like to adopt their child although their wishes cannot always be met.

Social services should give advice to parents to help them understand the court system. Social services must also provide an interpreter if the parent's or child's first language is not English.

Although the parents can change their mind at any time and withdraw their permission the court may well decide the parents are being unreasonable and can overrule them in order to meet the best needs of the child.

How long will it take and what will be different?

There is no set time and it will be different in every case. The child must have lived with the family for at least three months before adoption procedures begin.

- Most adopted children take the name of their new family.
- They will get the same rights and status as any other children in that family.
- They will gain extra family such as grandparents.
- They won't have a social worker, though they can still ask to see one but this is most unusual.
- They won't have reviews.
- If they want to, and it is appropriate, arrangements may be made for them to keep in touch with birth parents or other birth family members by letter, cards, photos etc. or sometimes by meeting, either in their new home or at a neutral place.
- They will get a new birth certificate with an adoption entry on it. When they are 18 they can apply to see their original birth certificate.
- If there has been no contact with their birth family they may decide at some time in their life to trace them, perhaps by joining the Contact Register.
- The new parents will be sent a letter explaining the adoption.
- An adoption order is a court order and the court hearing decides whether an adoption goes ahead. The Court may make some additions to the order for example to allow contact with certain people.

What are open adoptions?

Open adoptions are the same as traditional adoptions except that there may be anything from contact with birth parents or other birth relatives who are important to the child, an exchange of the occasional letters, cards or photographs to regular meetings.

Specific post-adoption services are available to give support and counselling, where requested, around the issues relating to adoption placements.

What if I want more information?

The following may be able to help (see pp 176–181 for more details):

- local social services office
- BAAF (British Agencies for Adoption and Fostering)
- Post Adoption Centre
- National Children's Homes
- National Organisation for Counselling Adoptees and their Parents (NORCAP)

Complaints

Children who are old enough to want to make a complaint may need a lot of help to do so. Carers should understand that making a complaint for a child is a positive step. It means the child has:

- thought about the situation
- decided that something is not right
- is willing to do something about it

There are two different types of complaints:

1. The really serious ones which must be handled formally.
2. Those which can be handled within the home, such as moans, suggestions and problems.

What may seem unimportant to you may be very serious to a child.

Complaints about sexual or racial harassment or racial discrimination are extremely important. You may be able to help or you may have to take the matter further.

If a complaint is made, an investigating officer will be appointed (Independent Person) as well as someone from the local authority management team. Separately, each will carry out an investigation.

Everyone should know what the complaints procedure is and how to go about making a complaint. If the information is not available the child should be helped to find out about the procedure.

Carers in children's homes and foster carers will have their own complaints procedure which may not be the same as the one for children.

Children may feel that it is not worth making a complaint, such as against their social worker, either because they might be victimised or because the system is stacked against them.

If the complaint is of a serious nature then the correct formal procedure for your authority must be followed.

Carers should keep the child informed of what is going on and let them know the outcome of the complaint.

Of course, carers may not feel able to help the child for all sorts of reasons. If this is the case, the child should be put in touch with someone who can. These might be:

- senior members of local authority staff
- Citizen's Advice Bureaux
- local councillors
- ombudsmen
- the courts via a solicitor—a child can ask for a judicial review

Some hints for handling a complaint:

- Listen attentively to the child's complaint. Make sure you fully understand it. Take notes.
- Show that you understand their feelings and thank them for raising the matter.
- State your own position undefensively and without hostility.
- Find out if the child has any suggestions for resolving the complaint.
- If appropriate, say that you will do your best to correct the situation.
- Always set a specific follow-up date.
- Always give the child a copy of your notes or a copy of the formal complaint.

Discrimination

Many different people are discriminated against for a wide variety of reasons. Because they are:

- fat
- old
- young
- female
- gay
- disabled
- 'in care'
- have different ways of doing things
- work hard at school
- don't like sport
- white in an area where there are mainly black people
- black in an area where there are mainly white people

Discrimination of all kinds is wrong. Discrimination is offensive.

Why do people discriminate?

Some people discriminate because they do not like a particular group or situation; sometimes they just do not understand the different culture or the disability. Many people discriminate without realising it.

Most black children who were born in this country have British nationality and have the same rights as everyone else. Some white children often don't understand this.

There are comparatively few black people living in this country (about seven per cent of the population) so when white children, from mainly white areas, meet black people for the first time it can come as quite a culture shock. However this has been lessened recently because there are lots of black people on television.

Discrimination doesn't just mean treating someone differently, it also includes using names, or words, no matter how innocently, which put people down. If you hear name-calling going on, ensure you discuss it. All too often children don't realise how hurtful and cruel they are being.

Children often do not understand what the words they are using mean. It is usually something they have heard others say.

Am I black or am I white?

'Am I black or am I white?'
I used to ask that question
every day and night
why do you ask a question
as obvious as that?
It's plain to see that you are black

But being in care
In a white Community
It's hard to decide
With no black family

These are the first two verses of a poem by Margaret Parr in *Black Experiences of Improving Practice with Children and Families*. It highlights the problems of a black child being cared for by white carers.

What does the law say?

The law says that due consideration should be given to the child's religion, racial origin, cultural and linguistic background and that the local authority must provide services to help disabled children to lead the lives they wish.

What does this mean:

Recognising differences
Differences should not be ignored. People are not all the same. Some people have different skin colour, hair, religious backgrounds. They may practice different rites in relation to their culture. Some children have different languages. Some children may be in a wheelchair or have a speech impediment.

Respecting differences
No one should be discriminated against because of their difference. Children may need your help to learn to respect these differences.

Meeting racial, disability, religious, cultural, dietary and cosmetic needs
Children may previously have been living with their own families or have been looked after away from their families. As their carer, you will need to find out what the child has been used to and what practices they would like to follow or what practices their parents would like them to follow. The child may have views on whether or not they want, for example, to eat Asian, Caribbean or Scottish food; attend a Mosque, West Indian or Catholic Church; wear their hair in a particular way; be treated differently because of their disability.

Children may:
- want to know if they can buy certain foods or cream for their hair or skin
- need to know where to buy particular tapes if they are visually impaired or to find out how to get access to different places if they are in a wheelchair
- need support and help to explore different possibilities for their life
- need help so they feel confident about asking for and getting assistance

Language

The language we use to describe ourselves, and others, can be very important in establishing self-confidence and identity. In the UK at present, the term 'Black' is often used to cover a wide group of people of different ethnic origins. However, some people do not like this collective term and prefer their individual nationality to be used, e.g. Chinese, Asian. The term 'Black' has been used by some as a political term of unity. You may feel it appropriate to discuss this with the children in your care.

How can carers help?

- By giving support. Sometimes children may suffer harassment. They will need help and guidance in all sorts of ways, for example, on how to complain and to whom to complain.
- By building pride and esteem. All children need positive images of themselves, their background and way of life.
- Find out all you can about the background, history and culture of any child who lives with you. It may be something you could do together. Local libraries are a good starting point for this research, so is talking to the child and their family—see also p 45 on Culture and Religion.
- Discuss with the child and parents what food the child likes to eat and then explore together the shops that sell such foods.
- Discuss with parents, ideas and information about how to deal with racism and discrimination.
- Ask the parents or find out the names and addresses of play groups or local youth groups where children can meet other young people of their own culture or religion or other disabled children if they wish.
- Carers should ask for training on how to cope and how to help the child cope with discrimination.
- Carers' support groups could discuss discrimination and carers could help each other with practical suggestions on how they coped with past situations such as racist neighbours or name calling by other children.
- Carers should also think very carefully before taking responsibility for a child from a different culture. How does my family feel? What problems might there be? Will I be able to cope?
- It is also very important that carers challenge discrimination about being in care.

Example

Verity told us that her teacher assumed that because she was in care she had very little money. He said that she didn't have to take part in a fund raising event. She was really very cross. Verity and her sister both said that what is needed is publicity about being in care so people know and understand. 'Everyone thinks we've done something wrong, we're dishonest or very poor.'

Discrimination should be challenged at every level at all times.

Activity 1: The houseboat children

The following true story is about three children who are fostered and then eventually adopted. All the names have, of course, been changed.

At the end of the story are some questions a carer might like to work through with the child. Older children might like to work on their own talking about the answers with their carer later. The answers are in the story and in other parts of the book.

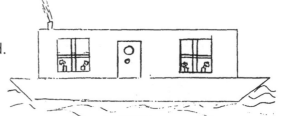

Chapter 1—Leaving their family

Joe, Molly and Sam lived on a boat with their mummy and daddy. They were four, three and two years old. They didn't have any friends except each other because their daddy moved the boat from place to place looking for work. Sometimes when they were very poor he even sold their toys.

One day their mummy became very ill. She couldn't look after them as she had to go to stay in hospital. They were all very sad as they missed their mummy very much. Their daddy told them that he couldn't look after them as well as he would like to do. Although he was very upset he had decided it was best for everyone if they were looked after by social services.

Joe started to cry blaming himself for making his mummy ill. Joe thought that because he had been naughty recently that was what had caused the illness. His daddy of course told him that it was definitely not the case. His mummy had been ill for some time but had not told anyone.

A few days later their daddy telephoned and asked if someone from social services could look after the three children until their mother was better.

A social worker called Liz came round and talked and talked to their daddy. He then signed a piece of paper, gave Liz a bag in which were a few clothes belonging to the children. He then gave Joe, Molly and Sam a big hug and told them to be good. None of the children really knew what was going on but they were very excited as they were going in a car. They had never been in a car before.

The social worker called Liz seemed very nice. She took them to a large building in the middle of the city. There were toys to play with and Liz gave them a drink and some biscuits.

Chapter 2—Being fostered

Liz asked Joe and Molly lots of questions and then a doctor came to see all of them. Two other people came and there was lots of talking. Liz then made two or three telephone calls. All the time the children played happily with the toys.

Liz then explained that the three of them were going to be fostered. She told them they would stay in the house of Jan and her family who would look after them for a while. Jan would be their foster carer.

They were very excited. They were going in Liz's car again and then they were going to sleep in a house. None of them had ever slept in a bed before, only bunks in the boat. Liz gave Jan their bag of clothes which Jan put in a safe place.

So many new things happened to the children that they were very happy at first. Jan was very kind and so were her children. But then Joe started to get sad because he missed his mummy.

One day Liz and a senior social worker came to the house. After talking to Jan in the kitchen they all came out looking very glum. Liz told the children that their mother had died. Molly and Sam were really too young to understand properly but they kept very quiet.

Liz then told the children that their father had left a note saying he loved them but couldn't look after them. His boat was gone and no-one knew where he was. Lots of people had tried very hard to find the children's father but he seemed to have disappeared. The children were so upset they didn't know what to do. Molly went out in the garden at first. She didn't talk to anyone for several days. Joe cried a lot and kept saying it was all his fault. Because Joe cried, so did Sam.

Jan and her family were all very quiet and sad about the boat children's mummy and daddy but gradually Joe, Molly and Sam were not sad all the time. Jan talked to them whenever she could and they asked her all sorts of questions about their mummy's death and about their daddy.

All the children loved Jan; she was warm and kind. She gave them lovely food to eat. She told them stories and played games with them.

Chapter 3—Being adopted

When Liz told Joe, Molly and Sam they might not be able to stay at Jan's for long, Joe began to cry. Because Joe cried, so did Molly and Sam. They all cried. They were very sad.

When they were a little calmer, Jan told them that what she wanted was the very best for them. She told them a story about when she was a child and how she had been adopted. She told them what being adopted meant and that their social worker would be looking for just the right family for them.

Some time later, Liz told them that social services had found a family who wanted to adopt all of them. She knew quite a lot about this family; Liz thought they would all get on well. Liz then told Joe, Molly and Sam about this new family. They were coming round for tea the next afternoon.

The people who wanted to adopt them were called Simon and Jill. They didn't have any children of their own.

Jan had made a big cake for tea. She had let Joe put lots of cherries on the top and Molly and Sam had been given a little of the left-over icing to eat. Everyone was very excited.

Liz brought Simon and Jill to the house and introduced them to everyone. They stayed for about an hour.

Simon and Jill came again a few days later on their own and on the third visit took Joe, Molly and Sam to the park. Liz came the next day. She had been to see Simon and Jill first to see whether they liked the children, which they did. She then asked Joe, Molly and Sam whether they liked Simon and Jill.

It was then arranged for the children to go to stay at Simon and Jill's house for two days the next weekend. This seemed like an adventure and everyone was very excited. The weekend was a happy time too.

Not very long afterwards Joe, Molly and Sam went to be looked after by Simon and Jill. They were very sad to leave Jan and her family and everyone there was sad to see them go but they all knew it would be the best for the children. Jan did a special tea for her own family, Joe, Molly and Sam and their new family as a sort of celebration because Jan and her family knew they would miss the children.

Whilst the children were living with Simon and Jill, social services were doing a lot of work making sure everything would work out for the best both for Simon and Jill and for Joe, Molly and Sam. Liz also called to see them regularly.

Another social worker came once a week to see the children. She was called Sylvia and she helped each of them work on their life book. Simon and Jill also helped. Sylvia talked to the children, asked them questions, got them to draw pictures and took them to visit the place where their boat had been. They also took some photographs.

Jan had given Jill the bag of clothes the children had brought with them and also lots of photographs she had taken whilst they were fostered with her. The children stuck the photographs in their life book and asked Jill to keep the clothes in a safe place as they no longer fitted them.

In this way Joe, Molly and Sam had a record of what their lives had been like. They could tell their new family and friends and one day show their own children what their life had been like.

After a long time Simon and Jill told Joe, Molly and Sam that arrangements were being made for a hearing at the court to sort out the details for adoption. This was the final step—Joe, Molly and Sam became the legally adopted children of Jill and Simon.

Although the children would never forget their own mummy and daddy or Jan and her family they knew they would be very happy with Simon and Jill.

Activity 2: Questions and answers on fostering and adoption

1.   What does being fostered mean?

2.   Why were Joe, Molly and Sam fostered?

3.   Why else might children be fostered?

4.   For how long are children usually fostered?

5.   Who are foster carers?

6.   What does being adopted mean?

7.   Who wanted to adopt the boat children?

8.   Who can adopt children?

9.   Why are children adopted?

10.   How long does it usually take to become adopted?

11.   What is an adoption panel?

12.   What is a guardian ad litem?

13.   What is a life book?

14.   Who owns it?

15.   Why do some children make a life book?

All the answers to these questions are in this book

Activity 3: Wordsearch

1. Put a ring around the words shown
2. Find the page in The Foster Carer's Handbook where these words are written
3. Ask your carer if you don't know what any of the words mean

discriminate	accommodated	planning meeting
social worker	carer	review meeting
fostering	complaint	independent visitor
education	values	court order
health	exercise	religion
life skills	complaint	key worker

```
z  y  x  p  q  r  n  o  b  a  c  e
a  c  c  o  m  m  o  d  a  t  e  d
e  a  x  e  o  i  k  m  o  q  r  r
d  i  s  c  r  i  m  i  n  a  t  e
u  b  d  f  e  j  y  n  p  t  s  l
c  e  c  b  r  h  a  x  w  u  v  i
a  h  g  m  e  e  t  i  n  g  j  g
t  m  g  d  v  a  f  n  g  l  o  i
i  p  n  n  i  l  l  d  k  k  q  o
o  v  i  s  e  t  q  e  r  e  a  n
n  u  n  x  w  h  h  p  b  y  b  e
a  t  n  w  o  y  e  e  t  w  a  x
s  c  a  r  e  r  a  n  f  o  d  e
o  o  l  e  k  c  l  d  h  r  o  r
v  u  p  e  l  e  t  e  g  k  p  c
a  r  o  t  x  t  h  n  s  e  t  i
l  t  n  v  i  s  i  t  o  r  i  s
u  o  r  d  e  r  p  n  c  o  n  e
e  r  f  o  s  t  e  r  i  n  g  p
s  j  s  c  o  m  p  l  a  i  n  s
p  l  i  f  e  s  k  i  l  l  s  o
```

Section 4: Culture, Values, Beliefs and Religion

Culture

Everyone has their own culture. Culture has nothing to do with the colour of our skin. It is about the influences around us that make us the people we are.

Sometimes people move away from, or are born away from, the place of their heritage. It is important that they have the opportunity to learn about their own culture so they may make up their own mind about what influences they wish to affect their lives.

A neighbour of mine is from Scotland although he has not lived there for many, many years. He speaks with an extremely broad Scottish accent, mainly eats Scottish food and at every opportunity, wears his kilt. As someone who visits Scotland regularly to visit family and friends, I don't know anyone as 'Scottish' as John. You may know of similar examples from people of other countries.

It is natural that people who understand and love their own culture should want to share this with others. It is also natural that young people should want to develop their own culture based upon the life they wish to lead.

Tolerance is the key here. Tolerance to respect not just other people's culture and heritage but their beliefs and religion as well.

Tolerance to accept that, just because our own culture is special to us, it may not be special to others. Tolerance and patience to learn, and understand, about other people's lives and influences. Tolerance in accepting this knowledge and way of life, whilst not necessarily agreeing with everything.

Values

Most people agree that it is important to have a set of values or beliefs to help and guide us through life. Our values and beliefs help us to decide what is right or wrong and how to behave in certain situations.

We get our set of values—the **dos and don'ts** of life as we grow up. Some we get from the family we grow up with, some we get at school, some we learn at play and others we learn from friends and other people who influence us.

Some people get their set of values from religion. That is what religion is, a set of beliefs or values that influence a person's life and behaviour. Religion is personal to each individual.

There may be others who share these beliefs and values. There will certainly be others who do not do so. There will be others who have no religion at all but they will certainly have their own beliefs and values.

Beliefs and religion

People who have like-minded beliefs sometimes join together to form an organised 'established' religion. Some of these world religions are:

Buddhism	Chinese religions	Christianity	Hinduism
Islam	Judaism	Sikhism	

Religion means different things to all these groups of people. Within each religion, there are likely to be different sects with different beliefs and levels of commitment.

A religion needs continuity and rules to give it strength. It also needs to grow and change to the ideas and needs of a new generation and an ever changing world.

We all need to be understanding and respectful of each other's religions, customs, symbols and places of worship.

On the following pages there is a brief guide in alphabetical order to the most well-known religions as they seem to be practised in this country.

There is an excellent series of books that can be used with children. The series is called *Open Sez Me* by Shirley West. There is a book for each of the seasons. Each book contains things to do; poems, songs, stories, recipes, facts. There is also a list of the important festivals that are celebrated by the different religions.

Buddhism

Buddhism is a philosophy, or way of thinking, rather than a set of social rules. Belief in re-incarnation encourages a Buddhist to lead a good life. The name Buddha means 'enlightened one'.

There are many Buddhist sects, but all follow the five laws (silas):
1. No killing
2. No stealing
3. No sexual misconduct
4. No falsehoods
5. No drinking of intoxicating substances.

Buddhism shows a love for all living beings and respect for all forms of life. Charity, hospitality and self-discipline are encouraged.

The Buddhist goal is to escape the eternal cycle of life and death and to reach a state of perfection—'Nirvana'.

Religious observances: Buddhists worship in temples in which are huge statues of Buddha. The monks and nuns shave their heads and wear yellow robes.

Buddhist festival: late May–early June: Wesak.

Worship consists of meditation and chanting. Incense and candles are often burned and flowers offered. Some Buddhists fast on the first and 15th day of each lunar month (between the new and full moon). Fasting may just mean no meat eating, but is a matter of personal choice.

Diet: no regulations; but the majority of Buddhists are vegetarians.

Birth customs: nothing specific is laid down.

Death: cremation is preferred.

Christianity

Christianity is named after Jesus Christ who is considered by his followers to be the Son of God, made man, but also God in His own right.

There are many sects of Christians in all countries in the world. As Christianity spread to different parts of the world, each country accepted its main beliefs. Each country added its own culture and way of doing things to the forms of worship that were already established. The result is a world-wide religion and following of people whose beliefs are similar. The only difference is that the ways of worship vary from country to country and even church to church in the same country.

Some Christian churches are Baptist, Catholic, Methodist, Presbyterian, Church of England, Ireland, Scotland and Wales.

As Christ himself was a Jew, the early Christians used a lot of readings from the Old Testament, and psalms and hymns from the Jewish faith.

As Christ's preachings and his follower's letters and accounts of his life were gathered together they formed the 'New Testament'. The 'Old' and 'New' joined together and became known as the Bible or Holy Book of the Christians.

Religious observances: the central beliefs of Christianity are:
- there is only one God—his son, Jesus, died and rose again from the dead
- the keeping of the Ten Commandments
- there is resurrection, a life after death, with God for all time

God consists of three people in one—Father, Son and Holy Spirit.

Some Christians also have a great respect for, but do not worship, Mary, the Mother of God, or other holy men and women as Saints.

Christians gather in churches to worship. Their holy day is Sunday.

Abortion is not encouraged by the Christian churches. Some, notably the Roman Catholic Church, forbid abortion and birth control.

Diet: no restrictions except on special fast days, e.g. Good Friday for some people.

Birth customs: after birth Christians are baptised —some shortly after birth, some at an age when they understand what is involved. At baptism a child may be totally immersed in holy water or the sign of the cross may be drawn in holy water on the forehead.

Confirmation is when a young person agrees to accept the laws of the church and promises to try to uphold them.

Marriage: is considered binding but divorce is granted in some circumstances.

Death: a person may be attended by a senior churchgoer, or leader such as a priest or vicar who will be with the person as they near death or as they die. Cremation and burial are both permitted. Christians believe very strongly in the resurrection, or rising again, of the body and soul joined together in God and in eternal life.

Hinduism

Hinduism is the most established of the world's religions. It is not based on the teachings of any one special person.

Hinduism is a social system as well as a set of religious beliefs. Hindu practices vary a great deal depending on caste and areas of origin.

Caste is inherited by birth and is determined by individual Karma, meaning reward for good deeds and punishment for wickedness. There are four main groups:

1. Brahmin—priestly caste; who teach and perform religious ceremonies and encourage others to learn religious duties
2. Kshatriya—military caste; who protect society and govern, rule and administer a country to lead a disciplined life
3. Vaishya—who engage in business, trade, commerce and agriculture
4. Shudra—the manual labourers

Hindus in Britain may observe the caste system and wish to avoid dining or inter-marriage with members of other castes.

The five main rules or principles for Hinduism are known as the five 'P's, which translated mean (1) God, (2) prayer, (3) re-birth, (4) law of action, (5) compassion for all living things.

The four things to work for are:
- religious duties
- satisfaction of desire
- material prosperity
- salvation

Religious observances: Hindus pray twice daily. They may use holy books, prayer beads and burn incense. At home a shrine may be set up sometimes in a room set aside for prayer. The temples are used for festivals and special celebrations. Horoscopes are an important part of religious belief.

Fasting is practised by devout Hindus, mainly women. Some Hindus may fast weekly, depending on their loyalty to a particular deity or the position of the stars.

Fasting to Hindus means eating only pure foods such as fruit/yoghurt.

Diet: many Hindus are vegetarian. Beef, as cows are sacred, or pork, as pigs are scavenging animals in India, are never eaten by Hindus. Some do not eat eggs—they are seen as a source of life—or cheese if it is made with animal rennet.

Onions and garlic are seen as harmful stimulants. Some Hindus avoid tea and coffee. Alcohol is officially frowned upon.

Special customs: spiritual purity and physical cleanliness are extremely important.

Most Hindus prefer showers to baths. Modest dress is favoured for both men and women. Women may wear a Sari, loose fitting trousers, a top and a long scarf covering the head (Chadar). Men must cover themselves from waist to knee. Women would not expect to undress fully for a medical examination and would prefer to be examined by female medical staff.

Gold worn next to the skin is believed to protect the wearer from many diseases. Married women traditionally wear a gold brooch and bangles. They usually wear a small coloured, red 'bindi' or spot on their foreheads. They may also put red along the parting of their hair in the early years of marriage.

Men of the Brahmin caste may wear a holy thread (janeu) over the right shoulder and round the body. It is both religiously and culturally very important and most men would be reluctant to remove it.

Birth: after birth the holy symbol 'Om' is written in honey on the baby's tongue by a close relative. The baby's horoscope is read and the birth celebrated six days later.

Family planning: no specific ruling. Abortion is frowned upon, but individual attitudes vary.

Some Hindu women prefer not to leave the home for 40 days after giving birth.

Death: cremation is preferred.

Traditional medicine: 'Ayurvedic' practice is complementary to conventional health care. The practitioners are known as 'vaids'.

Islam

Muslims believe in one God. They accept all prophets and their books but recognise the prophet Mohammed (PBUH) as the latest prophet. The Prophet's name is always followed by the words 'Peace be upon him' or PBUH.

Religious observances: worship is in a Mosque. The holy book is called the Koran and Friday is the Muslim's holy day. Islam has no caste system, it is a belief intended for everyone.

Muslims are required to:
- pray five times a day—prayers are preceded by ritual ablutions or washings
- fast from dawn to sunset for one lunar month each year. This is known as Ramadan and is a moveable period. Fasting is waived for menstruating, pregnant and breast-feeding women; children who have not reached puberty; people who are ill or on a journey. In the last case, the lost days must be made up later
- give two and a half percent of their savings for the needy
- make a pilgrimage, or journey, to Mecca, the Holy City, once in their lifetime if health and money permit

Muslims should wash hands, face and feet in running water before prayer whenever possible.

Care should be taken that the toilet itself is not facing Mecca—the south-east as this would be seen to be disrespectful. Muslims pray facing Mecca and prefer to have a special room set aside for prayer. Shoes are not worn in this room.

Diet: Muslims may not eat the flesh of pigs; be this pork, ham or bacon. Other meat may be eaten provided it is killed in the manner laid down by Islamic law. This meat is called Halal. There are special butchers where this meat is sold.

Halal food should not be stored or cooked with non-Halal food. The cooking of Halal foods should be in separate containers.

All alcoholic drinks or dishes containing alcohol are forbidden, as are tobacco and drugs.

Special customs: these may vary according to area and degree of adherence to tradition.

Dress: men must be covered from navel to knee; only the hands and face of women should be seen.

Girls after puberty should be allowed to cover their heads or wear a veil in school, college or workplace. Sexes are kept apart until marriage; single sex education is preferred.

Pre-marital and extra-marital sexual relationships are forbidden. Mothers giving birth outside marriage are liable to be rejected by the community. Nakedness is considered shameful. Medical treatment by a person of the same sex is preferred.

Birth customs: the Azan, or call to prayer, is recited after the birth.

Family planning: there is no specific Islamic ruling against contraception, but it is disapproved of by custom. Abortion is frowned upon, but tolerated for medical reasons.

Male circumcision: all Muslim boys must be circumcised before puberty, any time from eight days to eight years, according to local custom.

Female circumcision: although practised in some Muslim countries, is not a Muslim religious practice.

Death: a dying Muslim should be turned to face Mecca (south-east). The Koran is read aloud. After death, because the body is considered to be the property of Allah, it must be in the care of Muslims. After washing, the body is dressed in a white shroud. The body must be buried in a Muslim cemetery 24 hours after death. Cremation is forbidden. The anniversary of the death is marked by giving of alms to the needy on behalf of the dead person.

Medicine: some traditional herbal medicines and medical practices are used together with conventional health care by some Muslims.

Judaism

The word God is never written in full in Judaism. Hebrew is the language of prayer.

A Rabbi is a Jewish leader, priest and teacher. The Jewish community considers itself to be both a religious community and an ethnic group.

Religious observances: Jewish practices are laid down by the Torah in the Talmud, which are the first five books of the Bible as interpreted by rabbis.

There are different groups of Jews—Orthodox, Reform and Liberal—all of whom observe these rules in different ways.
- The Sabbath or Jewish Holy Day, starts at sunset on Friday and ends on Saturday evening. Orthodox is very strict. Orthodox Jews may not do any kind of work on the Sabbath, not even switching on a light or electrical equipment, driving or using public transport; cooking, telephoning or writing—unless any of these is necessary to save life.
- Fasting for 25 hours beginning at sunset on the eve of Yom Kippur (Day of Atonement); and other specified days.
- Circumcision—nearly all Jewish boys are circumcised by a qualified Mohel eight days after birth.
- At the age of 13 boys are accepted as full members of the community in a ceremony known as Bar Mitzvah. Girls are accepted at the age of 12 with a Bat Mitzvah.

Dress: modesty is an important religious issue. Orthodox men keep their heads covered with a skull cap (Kappel) and the strictly Orthodox Jews wear a prayer shawl. Phylacteries (small, leather boxes containing biblical texts) are also worn except on the Sabbath.

Women wear sleeves below the elbow and hemlines below the knee. They may also wear a scarf or wig (scheitel) in public.

Children after the age of eleven should be educated in single sex schools.

Hasidic men will not shake hands with women and prefer not to look at them or speak to them.

Diet: these laws are observed to varying degrees by all practising Jews.

- The very religious will not eat before morning prayers, which may take up to 30 minutes.
- Pork and all things made with it are forbidden; so are shellfish, rabbits and birds of prey and some cheeses.
- Kosher is a word used to describe meat that has been killed and prepared according to Jewish law; or to any allowed food, e.g. all fruit and vegetables.
- Orthodox Jews are not permitted to eat meat and dairy products within several hours of each other and must use separate plates and utensils. Orthodox Jews must not take non-kosher medication unless there is no alternative.
- For the eight days of Pesach (Passover) no leavened bread, cakes or biscuits are eaten.

Birth customs: childbirth is always considered a life-threatening situation. After the head has been delivered the child is considered to be a separate human being whose life may not be sacrificed even to save the mother's life.

Family planning: some orthodox Jews forbid contraception and abortion unless the mother's health is at risk.

Mothers are excused fasting for seven days from the onset of childbirth. Until the 30th day they only have to fast on Yom Kippur (provided they are well).

Death: Jews must be buried on the day of death or as soon as possible afterwards. Cremation is forbidden by Orthodox Jews.

Sikhism

Religious observances: Sikhs or learners were remakers of combined aspects of Islam Hinduism. They originated in Punjab, India in the 15th Century. Guru Nanak was their leader and with his nine successors is revered as a saint.

The Sikh Holy Book is called the Guru Granth Sahib. Sikhs worship together in temples. The most famous of these is the Golden Temple at Amritsar. The river Ganges is held to be a sacred river. Sikh homes may have a shrine for the Holy Book. This may be in a special room. If so, shoes should not be worn in this area and the head should be covered. Prayers are said around sunrise and sunset. Saihajdhari are Sikhs who are striving towards Baptism. Amritdhari (baptised) Sikhs are very strict about diet, dress and prayers.

Dress: Amritdhari have a strict code of dress, known as the five Ks—in translation these mean:

1. Cutting of hair is forbidden.
2. A comb secures the hair.
3. Men wear a turban; women keep their hair covered.
4. A metal bangle is worn on the right wrist. A small symbolic dagger is carried.
5. Men wear short under-breeches.

Sikh men should not be asked to remove their turbans. Girls should be provided with Shalwar (or loose fitting trousers) instead of skirts and track suits for PE. They may not be permitted to go swimming after the age of 12 years.

Diet: beef, alcohol and tobacco are forbidden. So is Halal meat. Chicken, lamb or pork may be eaten. These should be killed according to Sikh rites (Chattaka). Many Sikhs are vegetarian.

Birth: is celebrated by a thanksgiving at the temple. After 13 days the baby may be baptised into the order of Khalsa by five Sikhs in the presence of the Holy Books, at home or in the temple. Sweets are given out to celebrate a boy's birth.

Mothers are required to rest for 40 days after childbirth and are given rich food. They are forbidden to prepare food during these 40 days.

Death: readings from the holy book are given by a reader from the local temple or a relative. Non-Sikhs may help the family to lay out the body if asked to do so, but the family is considered responsible for these rites.

Cremation is mandatory. The ashes are sprinkled on running water; in India the river Ganges would be considered the best.

Activity 4: Values, beliefs and religion quiz

Find out the symbols for the different religions and draw them—you may need to go to the library or to ask someone you know who has a particular religion.

What are your set of values? Answering the following questions may make you think what type of person you are:

	Agree	Don't agree
It is wrong to steal		
It is important to believe in a god		
It is wrong to tell lies		
It is wrong to bully people		
People are entitled to hold religious beliefs		
It is wrong to swear		
Non-religious people are bad people		
It is wrong to cheat		
It is possible to be a good person without being a religious person		
All people are equal		
You should respect other people		
It is wrong to 'grass' on your friends		
You should obey the law		

Can you think of some other questions similar to these?

Your carer, parent, teacher and friends might like to discuss these questions and your answers with you.

Section 5: Emotional and Social Issues

Growing up

Children are growing up all the time. Mostly they won't notice the changes until they are about nine or ten when the bodily changes start to occur relating to puberty. This may be a little later for a boy.

Do you remember?
- getting large hands and feet and feeling so ugly
- developing breasts and having to wear a bra
- not developing breasts when everyone else was
- getting spots
- having greasy hair
- becoming clumsy and knocking things over
- blushing
- starting your periods
- not growing as tall as your friends

Some children may be upset if their physical or sexual development is slower than that of their friends. Disabled children may also be equally sensitive if their sexual development is delayed or disordered.

Black children may become very sensitive and want more information about their roots and identity.

Children can be extremely sensitive even if outwardly they may appear morose or cocky. There will be media pressure and peer group pressure for young adolescents to behave in a particular way.

One day they may act very responsibly and well, the next they will revert to being very childish or rude. The child probably won't know why they react or feel or behave the way they do.

Children at this time particularly need a warm caring environment, consistent handling, constant re-assurance, someone they can talk to about their worries, and someone patient who understands and respects the children's privacy. The most valuable thing you can give a child is your time; time to listen, time to talk, time to understand.

Decision making

We all know it's much easier to put off making decisions until tomorrow! Decision making is an important life skill which children need to learn.

Learning to make decisions can never start too early. However, very young children will need to have their choices directed or limited:
Would you like:

> juice or milk?
> chocolate or cheese?
> this jumper or that one?
> the park or the woods?

As children get older they can think about:

> what's best?
> why did that happen?
> what might happen if?
> if I do that, what then?

Everyone makes mistakes. Some mistakes are less serious than others. Some don't matter; some can be put right; some can never be put right. We can learn from the mistakes, so we don't make the same ones again.

What is important is that children have the opportunity to choose to do something. Even if the decision is wrong, they will learn from the experience.

You could talk to the child about how they feel afterwards. You could discuss what the other options were. What might have happened if a different decision had been made?

To make decisions children need to learn to:
- think about the situation
- take it steadily, not rush
- think about other ideas, which may come to them
- weigh up the possibilities
- think about what might happen
- sift and organise the facts and information they have
- if possible, experiment
- finally decide

The following are two ways that could be used to help the decision-making process. You could work through them with the child on a few minor issues at first. What is important is that the child learns not to make rash decisions and has a set way to work things out.

Activity 5: Decision making—The simple logical method

1. **Define**: What is the real problem? What is the cause? What am I trying to achieve?

2. **Collect the evidence**: Facts and figures.

3. **Generate ideas**: Make judgements, what do other people think? Look at the problem from different angles and alternatives.

4. **Plan**: What freedom have I got? What is the best thing to do for now? What is the best things to do for the future? How will it affect other people?

5. **Act**: Carry out what you have decided. Tell others what you are doing.

6. **Follow up**: Check that what happened was what you intended.

Activity 6: Decision making—The for and against method

Make a list of all the good points and all the bad points of making a particular decision. It is surprising when this has been done how easy the decision will seem. If there is more than one choice then the fors and againsts for each can be compared. The following is an example:

Choice—decide between	For	Against
Going on a school trip		
Going to Brownie or Cub camp		
Staying at home and going for day trips		

Encouraging positive behaviour

Behaviour is a way of communicating

With some children being difficult may be their way, often their only way, of telling you that they feel awful/angry/distressed about something or everything. Extreme behaviour is often related to extreme distress.

All carers try very hard to do what is best for the child. Yet sometimes it seems whatever they do fails.

A child psychotherapist, Miranda Passey, points out that children have an inner world which they have with them always. This is their own idea or view of people, experiences, events, and themselves.

Very often this view is quite different from reality. Sometimes this fantasy will greatly affect how the child experiences, includes, or rejects reality.

This means that some children will be difficult to 'reach' and may seem distant or defiant. Carers may be bewildered or baffled by this behaviour. The child may also try to provoke the carer into behaving the same way as their parents did; in a strange way causing the carer to fail them.

Children who are fostered often have a long history of failure and expect to fail, even sometimes try to fail. Using the 'Know Yourself' questionnaire on p 76 may help both the carer and child to learn more about the child. One girl when asked to list her worst points said 'lying'. Once she had accepted this, and brought it into the open, then she and her carer were able to work together to help her change.

Although it may sound impossible, when a child is being defiant or outrageous, if the carer can stop, look at what is being said or done, and ask themselves 'Why?' It may just help both the child and the carer.

When children have been particularly difficult, especially if this behaviour comes out of the blue, try to find out what is bothering them—not, of course, until they have calmed down. If children are reluctant to talk, the Worries Sheet may be helpful.

It is a good idea to make a note of when difficult behaviour occurs, to see if there is a pattern. For example, a child may be 'high' say every Tuesday, after school (hates the maths lesson). Someone else may be difficult after reviews or visits home. It is also worth noting when children are not being difficult. Carers can then speak to the child positively and look for ways of lessening the difficult behaviour.

The ABC analysis

By working out the pattern it will allow the carer to plan and prepare to counter or avoid the problems.

This sort of analysis is called the ABC Analysis.

A	**Antecedent**	—	what happens before the behaviour?
B	**Behaviour**	—	what actually happens?
C	**Consequence**	—	what happens as a result of the behaviour?

It is equally useful for positive behaviour as well as for difficult behaviour as it helps build up a picture of behaviour patterns and will help the carer to take action accordingly.

The influence of others

How often does it happen that the influence of others affect our own views of what is and is not acceptable? It might be politicians, the media, our next door neighbour or, of course, our partner. It is therefore important to think about exactly **what** is unacceptable behaviour and how that differs from what you are in fact getting. If the difference is negligible it will often be better to take no action, merely making a note of the occasion in case something similar occurs in the future.

Carers' values and standards

We all have different values, different prejudices, different standards. Before confronting a young person's unacceptable behaviour it is necessary to think about why the young person has behaved in a particular way. For example, a young person may eat with their mouth open, chomping their food and talking at the same time—perfectly acceptable behaviour in their own home but not necessarily so in the dining area. Should the young person be told? If yes, then when? Certainly, not at the meal table in front of others. Some would say we should not impose our own class values on the young people. Young people themselves will tell you they want to know how to behave to help them in the future. Another young person may be abusive when what they really mean is 'I can't do it, I need help'. They lack confidence.

The following are examples where behaviour may differ and the child may be unaware that their behaviour or action is unacceptable. Explanations and reasons may be all that is required:

- swearing
- drinking from a bottle
- keeping boots or shoes on in the house, putting feet up on chairs
- washing hands before or after using the toilet
- rushing to go through the door in front of others or letting the door slam
- helping or not with the washing up
- respecting a person for what they are regardless of their sex, sexual orientation, religion, race, culture, disability or ability.

Young people will also have varying morals about the same subject in differing circumstances. For example, they may see nothing wrong in stealing from shops or other people, yet if their sister was robbed the young person might well beat-up the thief and quite soon after decry violent behaviour at football matches.

So what can be done? It is essential children have opportunities to experience new situations, understand and be tolerant of other people's cultures and way of life; visit new places, have new challenges; take part in discussions. In this way they will learn from these experiences and develop their own principles and beliefs and at the same time learn to respect those of others.

The La Vigna model

This is a widely used behaviour management strategy which has five parts. All may be used or only one strategy may be necessary. For example lessening the noise in a room by switching the sound down on the television may cause a complete and sudden change of behaviour in the child.

The strategies are:

Environment change: moving the child to another room or changing the lighting, noise levels, crowding, or temperature.

Time: giving them time; time alone, your time and other people's time.

New skills: focusing on why the child behaves in a particular way and teaching them other ways of achieving the same ends. Ask yourself, and get them to ask themselves, what does this behaviour mean. It may be a coping strategy that the child has developed over time in response to their experiences, even though it may be an ineffective way of getting their needs met.

A new teacher said:

'I didn't realise that when a child said that it was stupid and a waste of time what they really meant was that they couldn't do it or hadn't understood. Once I realised that, I was better able to cope with and avoid these difficult situations.'

In this case the child needs to learn to ask, if not sure. They need to know that to ask is a strength not a weakness.

They also need to learn about the quality and quantity of relationships, respect and dignity and how to express their needs and emotions.

Reinforcement: for some children (and adults!) any attention is better than none. Sometimes adults unwittingly reward bad behaviour by giving the child extra attention. They fail to give reward or recognition to the good behaviour. The child thus feels as though they are being punished for behaving well.

Reactive strategies: the previous areas have focused on bringing about positive behaviour changes for the young person. Such a process will not, of course, work overnight. It will take time for the child to learn new skills and new behaviour patterns. In the meantime, it will be necessary to have planned strategies for responding to unacceptable behaviour.

Reactive strategies are not about improvements in behaviour but managing immediate situations in a way which seeks to avoid escalation into more difficult situations. For example:

non-verbal signal	*eye contact, frown, glare*
close proximity	*simply moving closer to the young person*
redirection, reward, praise	*that looks interesting, well done shall we try...*
active listening	*not assuming you always know what the difficulties are but genuinely listening to the child's views and reflecting their feelings back to them*
humour	*not sarcasm*
relocating	*suggest they move to another room*
ignoring	*sometimes ignoring the situation is the best strategy but being aware of early signs of escalation is vital*

Recap: It is possible to reduce inappropriate behaviour by:

- preventing the behaviour in the first place by arranging the environment so that opportunities for misbehaviour are minimised
- seeing what the aim of the problem behaviour is and replacing it by alternative methods of achieving this, that are easier for the young person and socially acceptable

What children should know about their behaviour

Children should be encouraged to discuss:
- their behaviour and others' behaviour
- right and wrong
- what is acceptable and what is not
- what control is needed and why
- what sanctions should be imposed, how and by whom. They need to believe the system in their home is fair and is applied across the board consistently
- their relationship with carers, teachers and other children and why they might feel aggressive towards them, frightened of them, impressed by them

Children also need to learn to aim for standards they can achieve. It is important that children learn to be responsible for their own behaviour and the consequences. Children must learn to be realistic.

> *'I want discipline. At my review I got what I wanted...I had got used to discipline...and there wasn't any. I asked to be disciplined. My brother asked to be disciplined.'*
>
> **Hampshire teenager**

Children really do want discipline. They want to know their carers care. They want to know how far they can go and what the consequences will be if they go beyond the boundaries.

In many local authority areas the term 'care and control' is used instead of 'discipline and punishment' but the children seem to prefer the terms they know.

The official guidance?

The following forms of punishment may not be allowed in children's homes:
- corporal (physical) punishment (except in Scotland—where there are strict guidelines)
- withholding food, drink and medicines
- restricting contact with family or social workers
- forcing children to wear clothing that is unsuitable
- depriving children of sleep
- withholding medical or dental treatment
- fines

With regard to punishment, foster carers are given similar powers as parent(s) under the law. They are permitted to enforce 'reasonable' discipline and punishment but they should take the above as guidelines.

With young children, a look, a glare or a touch on the arm may be enough to make them realise they are misbehaving. Carers also have to be sensitive and to know when to hold back. It may after all be the first time the child has really had fun and the offence isn't really that bad anyway!

Sometimes it is difficult to understand why a child behaves in a particular way. For example children may take food and hoard it. This may be because they are not used to the freedom of helping themselves; they are not used to having excess food or even sufficient food around; or purely to see the reaction of the carer. Talking over the situation is certainly the best tool here.

Children are often led on by other children without realising the consequences of their action. They might shoplift or play truant, thinking it's 'no big deal' and anyway 'I'll only get a caution'. Parents, carers, teachers, social workers, and the police may all be involved.

Together you could possibly draw up a form of contract agreeing acceptable behaviour and stating what will happen if the contract is broken. Another way to encourage positive behaviour is for the child to be set agreed goals, simple, easy-to-achieve ones at first.

A good carer will be aware of what is going on in the home and will often be able to defuse a situation just by being in the room, or in a doorway, or in the garden. However, if a child does have a tantrum, one carer told us that they run a 'time-out' system with a minute for each year of a child's age.

Angry or aggressive behaviour

If the child is very angry or aggressive then:
- don't have a slanging match, don't swear or shout
- think about what you say and don't stand in an aggressive way
- let them be angry. Channel that anger. Let them hit their pillow or whack the mattress. You could even give them a rolled up newspaper to do it!
- if they really are aggressive, try to move them to another room for their own safety
- **stay calm at all costs**—if you lose your temper, you may also frighten the child
- when the child has calmed down, wait for the right moment to talk to them
- **let them know you care**

Later, carry out an ABC analysis. It may be something you could do together.

Restraint

Restraint should be seen as an absolute last resort. Training should have been given in restraint techniques. The social worker should be immediately informed if it is necessary to use restraint and the carer should record all details meticulously. Any other appropriate procedures should also be implemented.

Once the situation has died down some of the strategies mentioned above should be used to try to find out:
- what caused the escalation of the situation
- what changes could have been made that might have prevented the need for restraint
- what changes need to be made in the future

Caring for yourself

Following difficult times such as these the carer should develop their own coping strategies in order to relieve stress; they might contact another member of a support group to talk over the situation.

They also need to be aware that there may be some negative comments and feelings from others and to have strategies and responses ready to deal with the situation.

Privacy and confidentiality

As children grow up they have a wish for secrecy; a desire for privacy and confidentiality. Many parents and carers find coping with this difficult, though this is a very natural part of growing up and should be respected. Children being looked after often hate the thought that they are talked about or that what they think they have told someone in confidence is being passed to someone else. They also hate to think that their file can be easily read by others.

We all want our privacy to be respected and children are no different. Children should be encouraged to knock on your bedroom door before entering and in return you should do the same to them.

Many carers and parents like to see things tidy. Yet children need their own space where they can leave things as they wish knowing they won't be gone through or examined.

Sometimes if you were to go through a child's belongings you might find drawings, writings or pictures you wished you hadn't seen or that will shock you. Usually this is just a normal part of growing up, finding out about their sexuality or expressing their feelings and emotions. They would possibly rather die than think someone had seen them.

Carers will also have their own personal belongings—respecting privacy should be a two-way process. Privacy and confidentiality can be a good area for discussion.

Some secrets cannot be kept—if you are worried that a child has suffered or is likely to suffer 'significant harm', you may have to take the matter further, but the child needs to know what you intend doing and why, and to be kept informed.

Self respect, self esteem and self confidence

Everyone needs to be valued, to feel special, to feel important. By treating looked after children as individuals, by working and caring for them you will build up their self confidence. By making opportunities for children to succeed you will build up their self esteem.

No matter what difficulties a child has had in the past, they need to know that you expect them to overcome these difficulties; that they must become responsible for their own life and behaviour. Treat them with respect and gradually they will learn to respect you and others around, and also to respect themselves for what they are. Children have to learn that real friends like them for what they are, not because they are slim or wear the latest fashion clothes. Sadly, children are often discriminated against because of their looks or their clothes. To have self respect and to build up confidence a child must understand and know themselves and what makes them 'tick'. Children must realise that they should take responsibility for their own actions.

At the end of this chapter is an exercise called 'Know Yourself'. Children might like to do this on their own, with you or in a group. It may help them to look at things with *fresh eyes*. If children show you their answers to the 'Know Yourself Quiz', you may be surprised, indignant or hurt but at least you may know the child a little better. The answers could also be used as a talking point.

Values

The various Children Acts and Orders were introduced to ensure that children are helped in all sorts of ways so that they learn to become responsible caring adults. Government advisers in schools have now issued a set of guidelines stating that teachers should work in **partnership** with parents or carers to see that children are able to make responsible decisions in their lives.

What this means is that both groups should be encouraging the children and expecting support from each other.

Children want this too. *'I want to know right from wrong'*, said a Hampshire teenager.

Children should learn to:

- know the difference between right and wrong
- tell the truth
- keep promises
- share
- respect the rights and properties of others
- act considerately
- help those less fortunate and weaker than themselves
- take personal responsibility for their actions and self discipline

What does all this mean? It means that you, as carer, will need to work with the children to help them develop their own sense of values.

They should also be taught to reject:

- bullying
- cheating
- deceit
- cruelty
- prejudice
- discrimination
- sexism
- gossiping

Many children complain if someone cheats on them yet a little later these same children will cheat on others. They need to learn about standards, about what is acceptable and what is not acceptable, and to think about how others feel and not just about themselves.

As they grow up children will become aware of issues such as:

- drinking alcohol
- loyalty
- divorce
- abortion
- bloodsports
- damage to the environment
- smoking
- sexuality

Group discussions, family discussions, reading newspapers and watching particular television programmes are all ways that can develop a child's beliefs. Children, however, should understand that other people may have different values from theirs such as religious and family values. These must be respected.

Of course, children will always question why things are as they are and will test the boundaries. There needs to be boundaries so children know where they stand, so they have something to rebel against and so that they have something to keep them in good stead for the future.

Identifying and dealing with abuse

Children who are looked after may have been abused in one form or another at some time in their life. Sadly, this may also occur during their time 'being looked after'.

What is abuse?

Physical abuse: where children are physically hurt, injured, given poisonous substances or drugs.

Ninety per cent of children who are physically abused have visible injuries, for example, bruises in places that do not normally get bruised by accident; or bruises of different ages; marks from beating; black eyes; burns or scalds, unexplained fractures and head injuries.

Physical abuse should be suspected where the explanation of the injury does not fit the facts, or if the child is reluctant to say how the injury happened.

Neglect: where a child's basic needs are not met such as food, warmth, medical care, shelter.

Emotional abuse: where a child suffers as a result of a constant lack of affection, verbal attacks, bullying, racial and other harassment, which undermine a child's confidence and self esteem.

Sexual abuse: where children are exploited by others to meet their own sexual needs. This may be sexual intercourse, fondling, masturbation, oral sex, anal intercourse and exposure to pornographic material including videos.

Common signs of sexual abuse are:
- injuries or soreness in sexual areas or mouth
- a wide range of emotional problems
- inappropriate sexual behaviour—overly sexual or extreme fear of intimate contact
- knowledge and understanding of sexual matters beyond their age

When it is suspected a child has been a victim of sexual abuse, they may be interviewed at a special safe place by trained staff, one of whom may be from the police. A video or tape recording may be made of this interview, so the child doesn't have to keep repeating their experiences. The child may be asked to have a medical.

What happens if a carer suspects abuse?

Where carers are concerned that a child has been abused, they should record their concern, share their concern with a social worker or senior member of staff. They should also consult their child protection manual. In some cases they may have to speak to someone outside their own organisation.

Breaking confidentiality is a big problem. Some children will tell you, begging you not to tell anyone else. If you have evidence that a child is being abused, then you **must** pass this on. You will have to explain this to the child. They'll hate you at first but will be relieved when they know that something is being done. Keep them informed.

How can carers help children who may have been abused?

- Listen to what a child says.
- Avoid asking too many questions or asking for unnecessary detail.
- Be alert and observant.
- Protect the child.
- Try to find out what a child is afraid of.
- Follow the procedures for protecting the child when they are in danger of serious harm.
- Tell the child what you are going to do and what will happen next.
- Never tell lies to the child.
- Be familiar with child protection procedures.

Who are the abusers?

Most children who have been abused are abused by those they know and even like—older friends, parents, relatives, carers, neighbours.

This is particularly difficult for the child to cope with as he or she does not want to cause a problem to those close to them. Nevertheless, action must be taken as the abuser may go on to abuse others. You will have to help the child to understand this and that what abusers do is wrong. It should be made quite clear that the child is in no way to blame.

What are the other signs of abuse?

Any of the following may be associated with abuse and may be symptoms of distress:
- poor or deteriorating school work
- reluctance to go to school or frequent early morning minor illnesses
- problems with sleeping, nightmares
- complaints of hunger, lack of energy, apathy
- possessions often 'lost', dirtied, destroyed
- desire to stay around adults or avoid adults
- reluctance to attend health assessments
- unhappy, withdrawn or isolated child
- a new tendency to stammer
- lack of appetite, or 'comfort eating'
- aggression
- constant attention seeking, over-pleasing or compliant behaviour
- indications of substance abuse
- attempted suicide
- running away from home
- low self-esteem

Unlikely excuses to explain any of the above, or refusing to give any reasons for the above should ring 'alarm bells'.

What are the effects?

Physical scars heal but many children take longer to recover from the emotional trauma. They usually need professional help. Children who have been sexually abused over a long period of time may have little understanding of what is appropriate sexual behaviour. This will have to be learnt. Carers must be aware of this and ensure that they do not place themselves in situations which could be misinterpreted.

Victims of sexual abuse may act out their abuse on younger children in the household. Carers need to be alert. Dealing with this may need particularly sensitive handling and carers may wish to ask for professional help.

What are a child's rights?

Children are entitled to be protected from all forms of abuse. Let them know they are not alone and that you are there to protect them. Many children will find it hard to talk about being abused; they need to know that you can be trusted, and that you will believe them. They need to know they are not to blame, but most importantly they need to know that some 'secrets' cannot be kept.

Check your local Child Protection Procedures for further details.

Bullying

Many children suffer really badly because they are bullied. Children who are bullied are entitled to be protected. They often don't tell anyone in case they are thought of as 'grassers'.

Many of the effects of abuse mentioned in the last chapter may apply to a child who is being bullied so carers need to be observant. Studies show that over half of all children say that they have been bullied at some time.

What is bullying?

Bullying may be said to be long-standing violence, physical or psychological, conducted by an individual or group and directed against someone who is unable to defend themselves in the situation.

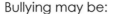

> *Bullying, Bullying*
> *it happens all the time,*
> *hitting and calling names*
> *you make out its fine*
> *but deep down you really hurt,*
> *you start to believe you're nothing but dirt*
> *but if you show them you don't care*
> *they'll leave you alone and forget you are there*
>
> **Emma Healey, aged 10**

Bullying may be:
- name calling
- physical violence including pushing, poking, pulling hair, punching
- gestures
- extortion—demanding money, food, homework, etc.
- exclusion from friendship

Who are the bullies?

Anyone:
- children of the same age
- older children
- dinner ladies
- caretakers
- swimming pool attendants
- teachers
- carers
- policemen
- parents

Sometimes younger children bully older children who are disabled or children who are quiet, nervous or shy.

James Tallack aged 10 told us:

> 'Bullying is most common around schools. There are always bullies in schools. They always hang around after school and before school starts. Sometimes people get bullied at playtimes and lunch times.'

> **If you or your friend get bullied, go and tell your teacher!**
> **If you are afraid of getting bullied, stay with your friends or family.**

Who gets bullied?

Anyone—but it seems that quiet, solitary and less aggressive children tend to get bullied more as do children who are smaller than their peers.

Bullying seems to occur around the age of ten years most often, mainly in the playground. Bullying seems to increase with the age of the child and is more damaging in secondary schools. Children with special needs and children from ethnic minority groups are twice as likely to be called names as other children.

What can children do if they are being bullied?

The following are some other suggestions for children who have been, or are being, bullied. Carers may like to pass these on or use them as a basis for discussion.

1. Suggest the child gets help, talks to someone they can trust such as their social worker, carer or someone at school.
2. If they are worried that telling will make matters worse, let them know that you will be discreet.

If it doesn't get sorted straight away, tell them not to give up. Schools should have an 'anti-bullying' policy so schools need to know what is going on. They must be very active in trying to combat bullying.

What else can children do?

Five useful tips:
1. **Don't let bullies think they are scaring you. Try to ignore or laugh at what they say—it's hard but worth a go.**
2. **If you do get angry, don't let it show.**
3. **Stay with a crowd—bullies usually pick on you when you're on your own.**
4. **Time your visit to the toilet at school so others are there too.**
5. **Keep a diary. Write down what happens each time you are bullied, what is said, when and where. Give this information to those who are helping you.**

> **No-one should tolerate bullying.**

> **Schools can do very little to prevent bullying unless**
> **they are told it is happening.**

Separation

Moving house

A child who is looked after may be separated from and miss:

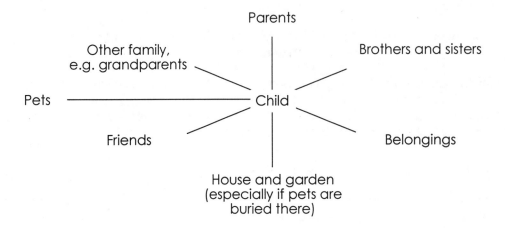

A child who moves from a residential or foster home back to their own home or to another home may be separated from and miss:

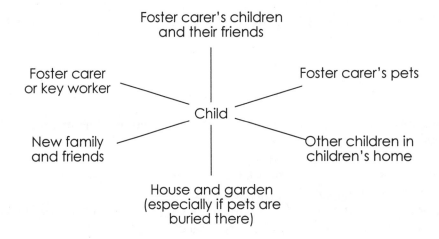

Moving house whilst living in a traditional happy family is said to be more traumatic to children than their mother having a new baby. How much more traumatic for the child who is looked after when they move away from the people they know and love.

This may be particularly difficult for children from an ethnic minority group who move to live with a family from a different background. These children may also move to an area where there are no other black children, adults or facilities such as Asian, Jewish or Caribbean shops.

How can carers help children who have to move?

- Have a warm welcoming environment for them.
- Get them to bring as much as they wish and can, including clothes, toys, mementoes.
- Carers can talk about themselves and about the others in the house to the children.
- If the children want to talk—**listen**. Don't ask too many questions.
- If children are moving on, tell them as much as you can about what to expect.
- Tell them you will be very happy for them to come to visit you.
- Some carers organise a celebration when a child is leaving. In this way it helps:
  - the foster carer's child to accept and come to terms with the leaving of the foster child that they have become fond of
  - the child to realise that they are important and that what is happening is for the best.

The loss experienced by a bereavement may be very similar for a child coming into care or for one who is moving on. The children may also blame themselves for what has happened.

Loss and bereavement

At any age losing someone or something you love even for a short time may be a very painful experience.

Talking and listening is the best tool for helping a child at this time but there are some practical things that can be done too.

It is sensible to introduce the idea of death from quite an early age:
  - a dead bird
  - a dying cat
- what does it mean?
- what causes it?
- what happens afterwards?

Carers could talk about the ageing changes that occur throughout life; how illnesses cause different changes; and why people die.

The child may not remember but if the time came when someone died, the words would at least be familiar. There are many books on the market that might help such as:

Grandpa by John Burningham
When Someone Very Special Dies by Marge Heegaard
Badger's Parting Gifts by Susan Varley
When Uncle Bob Died by Althea
Fred by Posy Simmonds
Water Bugs and Dragonflies by Doris Stickney

The story about Sarah and her pets (on p 86) might help too.

Death

If carers know someone close to the child is likely to die then the child should be prepared.

Carers might explain the meaning of words such as:
- death
- bereavement
- burial
- cremation
- funeral
- mourn
- cancer
- AIDS

If the child is old enough to understand, carers could also talk about the feelings and emotions of the different people involved; how different people will react in different ways.

When a death occurs, carers may also need to remind the child what the words mean and also explain, probably more than once, what is happening.

Rituals around death vary depending on the culture or religion. The carer may have to get more information so they can help and support the child.

What happens afterwards?

The better prepared children are, the more control they will have. The most common complaint of children bereaved is *'I wasn't included'*. (Frances Sheldon, Lecturer)

On hearing the news of the loss of someone they know and love children might feel a sense of shock and disbelief, a numbness.

This may be followed by:
- misery
- anger
- questioning
- sadness
- self-blame
- blaming others

If children know in advance that the loss is to occur they will have time to prepare themselves mentally. The impact of the loss is much greater if the loss is sudden.

When the time is right, talk to them or let them talk to you:
- talking helps to dispel wrong ideas
- talking helps to make good sense of the loss

Talk naturally or ask a question but don't put pressure on the child to talk. If they don't answer, accept this. Remember, even if they don't talk, the child is likely to be thinking about the dead person or may even be silently speaking to the dead person.

Children will feel pain. Let them. Don't try to make them get over it too quickly. There is no set time that bereavement lasts.

They will feel desolation and despair. They will feel there is no sweetness, no purpose, no point in their lives:

Who am I?   *What does it mean for me?*   *I'm an orphan.*
may be said many times.

The pain will recur again and again—at birthdays; anniversaries; at Christmas; at holiday times and at other times that were special for the particular family.

Some children may want to go to the funeral service, others may not. Some may want to visit the cemetery or crematorium, others may not. Whatever their wishes, these should be respected and if at all possible acted on. It may be necessary to check that the child understands the occasion if they wish to attend.

Carers may also need to be alert to rituals and symbols that different religions or cultures practise and use. *Caring for Dying People of Different Faiths* by Julia Neuberger may be useful. Help the child find practical things they can do, such as collecting mementoes or photographs or writing down how they feel.

You could perhaps suggest there is something they want to keep such as a sweater or a pair of slippers. Let them choose.

Remembering the person is important, so too, is feeling proud of that person.

Children can develop new relationships with others such as foster carers without destroying other relationships. Children need to know this; how to make room for that relationship; to realise that nothing will take the place of the person only that things will be different.

Losing a pet they have loved can be just as traumatic for a child as losing a loved one. Just buying a replacement probably won't solve the problem. Be open, be frank; talk and **listen**.

Divorce

The effect on children of divorce or separation is very much like that of death in many ways. They may be losing someone they love. The children often blame themselves. A child will need to be prepared for what is going on and be allowed to be involved in discussions if they are old enough to understand. A carer should not take sides.

A form of grieving may also take place. Be a good listener. Talk to the child. Be prepared.

Going into hospital

Separation also occurs when either the child, a parent, relative, close friend or carer goes into hospital. Whoever it is, the child needs to know why they or someone else is going into hospital. It is not a punishment. They are not being sent away. They are being taken to hospital to be made well again or to help ease their pain or because the doctor thinks it is best.

What should a child be told before going into hospital?

1. What will happen.
2. Explain that some people and children stay in bed all the time, have their meals in bed and use a potty in bed instead of going to the toilet.
3. Tell them who they will meet, doctors, anaesthetists, nurses, porters and other people who work in the hospital to look after people who are sick.
4. If children are going to have an operation simply explain that they will have a special sleep. When they wake up they will be sore, may have bandages on them but that they will gradually get better. If they are old enough to understand, you may, or the doctor may, give them more details. Tell them you will be there all the time they are asleep.
5. Be honest and accurate about how often you will see them and don't make promises about how soon they will be out of hospital.
6. Be calm and reassuring.

> **Never use going into hospital as a threat.**

In many hospitals it is now possible for the parent, carer or someone close to the child to stay with the child overnight. Social services can provide child care for the carer's own children or other foster children.

Permission for an operation must be obtained either from the parent or the social worker.

What should a child take if they are going to stay in hospital?

- toothbrush, toothpaste, hairbrush or comb, soap and flannel
- **clearly marked** dressing gown, night-gown, slippers and normal day clothes
- toys, games and books to remind them of home
- some young children may also want to take a comforter with them

What should a carer tell the hospital staff

- any particular words a child might use, for instance 'loo' or 'pee pee'
- any rituals a child may have for getting off to sleep
- special dietary needs
- medicinal needs such as an inhaler

How will the carer or the child know what will happen?

Most hospitals are much better than they used to be at explaining what will happen and what to expect. Many also provide useful booklets to read at home. If you have a worry or a query, please ask the nurse or doctor. They will be glad to explain anything to you.

What should a carer tell the child when leaving the child in hospital?

1. Tell the child they are going and when they will be coming back.
2. Tell the nurse when this will be so that they can comfort or occupy the child.
3. Never pretend they are going outside for a few minutes when they are actually leaving. This will cause the child even more stress.

The hardest part of all is leaving!

Some books the carer and child might read are:

> *Why, Charlie Brown, Why?* by Charles M. Schulz
> *When Someone Has A Very Serious Illness* by Marge Heegaard
> *When Your Mum or Dad Has Cancer* by Ann Couldrick
> *I Have Cancer* by Althea
> *When Someone Very Special Dies* by Marge Heegaard

Listening and being listened to

A good communicator should not lie or build up false hopes. They should be trustworthy, reliable and honest and most especially, a good listener.

You cannot listen to children all the time but you can often spot those who have something important to say by a change of behaviour or mood.

How can I be a good listener?

- Never be too busy to listen. Children have important things to say at the most inconvenient time of day.
- Listen to what is being said. Give the child your entire attention.
- Don't anticipate what will be said next. Wait and listen. That way you'll be sure.
- Keep your thoughts to yourself as to what is being said. Don't let your mind jump away from the topic.
- Pay attention to both what is being said and how it is being said.
- If you have a question, make a note of it unless it disturbs the child. Ask the question at the proper time. Don't interrupt or write while the child is actually talking. Asking questions can certainly help but they require careful handling and good timing.
- If you disagree, don't get angry. Wait until they have finished. They may say something that makes your anger unnecessary or even embarrassing.
- If the child is continuing for a long time, jot down a few notes when there is a pause or when they have finished speaking. This will help later on in remembering what was said.

A good listener will usually be listened to because they will have taken care to listen and will have thought about what they want to say.

> **Listening is as much an art as speaking; both require practice, both require attention.**

How can I be listened to?

- Plan the time and place to suit you both and if possible, tell the child in advance. Don't choose a time when a favourite TV programme is on!
- Plan what you want to say.
- Have a pen and paper ready to make notes.
- Tell the child at the start what you want to discuss.
- End by saying what is agreed and what action is to be taken.
- Show you are listening by eye contact, nodding or use of body language.
- Don't gossip or pass on what you have heard to others.

Respect confidentiality and privacy unless you feel the child is at risk of significant harm.

If you feel you must pass on something you have been told:

- tell the child, explaining what you will do and how you will do it
- explain **why** you are taking that particular course of action and when you will be doing so
- at all times help keep the child informed of what is happening
- be honest
- never make promises you can't keep

A child should know that the carer is always open and honest with the social worker.

Making and keeping friends

Friendship is a two way process. Some adults are unwilling or unable to make the effort to form friendships or help friends. This often relates back to their childhood.

We all need friends, so it is important that children have as many opportunities to make friends as possible. Friendship means:

- giving
- laughing
- confiding
- sharing

- taking
- joking
- talking
- being able to say sorry

- listening
- being with
- playing
- not gossiping

Friends are very important. Carers should:
- arrange lots of opportunities for the child to play with others
- help them to share and take turns with favourite toys and games
- try not to get involved if they argue; children can usually sort things out themselves
- be ready to offer sympathy and a listening ear afterwards
- make sure that the child has the chance to meet other friendly adults, too, and can answer them politely. Many children will make a special friend of an adult such as a grandparent

Many of the worries children mentioned (see p 79) relate to friendships:
- falling out with friends
- losing friends
- changing schools and missing friends
- moving on and not seeing friends again

Children need help to keep friends too. Carers could:
- invite friends to tea
- invite friends to stay the night
- get the child to telephone their friends
- get the child to write letters to their friends
- make sure a child who moves on leaves a new address and telephone number
- help the child organise a meeting of old friends
- allow the child to go to stay with a friend if that is possible

When a child first arrives at your home and you are being given information about the child, ask about the child's friends, who they are, and where they live. Try to help maintain these friendships.

Coping with a crisis

The word crisis conjures up different things to different people. To a small child it may be a crisis if an ear falls off a favourite teddy or they can't undo a tin or box. To an older child a crisis might be if their gran died or their pet cat was run over by a car. What is dreadful one day may be fine tomorrow.

Everyone is different and we all have our different ways of coping with crisis. Some children will wail and cry so it is obvious they have a problem, others will bottle it up. Their unhappiness may show with physical or psychological health problems.

Physical symptoms:
- feeling the heart is beating quickly
- pains and tightness in the chest
- indigestion and wind
- stomach pains and diarrhoea
- frequent passing of urine
- tingling feelings in the arms and legs
- muscle tension, often pain in the neck or low part of the back
- persistent headaches
- migraine
- skin rashes
- difficulty focusing
- lack of self-care and poor hygiene

Psychological symptoms:
- unreasonable complaints
- withdrawal and daydreams
- missing school
- accident-prone and careless
- poor work, cheating and evasion
- over-eating or loss of appetite
- difficulty getting to sleep and waking up tired
- feelings of tiredness and lack of concentration
- irritability

Many of these may be just normal growing-up symptoms but if they persist the child may have a problem.

What can a carer do to help them cope?

- let them know you care
- be available
- be a good listener
- re-assure them
- suggest positive steps such as:
  - talking to their friend, teacher or relative
  - taking part in a physical activity
  - giving themselves a treat
- make them feel secure
- help them become independent
- help them to look at things from all sides
- get them to have a medical check-up. Many problems vanish when they find they have nothing physically wrong with them
- if it's an emotional crisis, help them to cry. Have somewhere private so they can talk or cry without being heard or interrupted

Worries

The Sound of Silence by Emma J.C. Lauchlan aged 10 years

When we have a worry,
Silence is our sanctuary.
Silence is the Lady of the Night
Who comes along when we sleep.
She also comes when things are tense
And when we are sad.
When she comes, we don't have to speak,
Silence tells us what to feel.

If we let her speak for us, she will,
She will tell others how we felt
About someone or something.
Her voice carries high above
What we can say.

The father of Emma's friend died. She wanted to say how sorry she was but she didn't know how. She didn't say anything. She was silent. She then wrote this poem for her friend.

'A friend of mine has a problem…' or *'I know someone who…'*
If children start a conversation like that, that someone is often **themselves**!

All the time they can talk as someone else they won't get emotionally involved, they don't have to admit they have a problem and also they can go away and think about what you say without feeling under pressure.

Follow up quite soon by asking *'What happened?'* or *'Has your friend…?'*. You'll usually be told the truth then. If the matter is serious, get someone else to approach them if you feel you can't get any further.

We are all different and respond to people differently. Don't be upset if children tell their worries to someone else. Very few children are completely open with their own parents, never mind carers, preferring to talk to someone less closely involved with them, be it brother or sister, gran', neighbours, friend or teacher.

Something you and most of the world think is unimportant, may be really distressing to a sensitive child:
- be aware
- be patient
- be tolerant
- be honest
- be concerned
- be available
- be understanding
- be discreet

On page 79 is a list of problems children have said worried them. A child may like to go through the list and put a tick which says how they feel about things at that moment. It may help them to realise that they are not alone and that other children worry too. A child can add to the list anything else that is bothering them.

Talking and listening are the best tools for relieving worries. We all know that even the slightest worry can build up out of all proportion. Writing down their worries—the facts, the situation as they see it and what can be done about it, will often help. If a child shares worries with a carer, this will help them overcome them.

Carers also have worries. Other carers have shared their worries with us and we have listed some of them on pages 82–83. They too, may help you to realise just how similar your worries are to those of other carers.

Worries by Simone Brown aged 10

All my worries, all my prayers
Nobody cares
People bullying me.
Can't they see, I'm scared
I try to tell my parents
My brother and sister too,
But they just say,
Don't be stupid
I'm not listening to you.

All my worries, all my prayers,
Nobody cares.
I tell my best friend,
Who is in care.
*She said **they listen to me there**.*
I end up telling them my problems too.
*Now I don't worry, and neither should **you**!*

Becoming independent

When I was a teacher I took a group of 10–11 year olds on an educational visit to stay on an historic sailing ship. Prior to the visit we had regular sessions on navigating, knot tying, rowing, sailing, etc., in fact everything we could think of to make the expedition safe, enjoyable and beneficial.

What we had not realised was that less than half of these children had been taught basic independence skills. Very early on, one lad said, *'Please Miss, will you make my bed for me? My mum's very kind. She always makes my bed.'* I won't tell you my answer!

Hardly any of the children had experience of scraping the food off plates, of washing up, bed making, drying or changing their clothes if they were wet, without being told.

As soon as a child is old enough to understand, help the child to start to do things for themselves, such as:
- Getting things out for you or them.
- Opening boxes, lids, jars, pots.
- Putting things away.
- If they help with 'making pastry', show them how to clear up after themselves; to wash up and wash the work surface.
- Dressing themselves.

As a child gets older they should:
- Make their own bed.
- Keep their room tidy.
- Make toast and sandwiches.
- Pour soft drinks and serve them to others too.
- Put their clothes away correctly.
- Decide whether they need a coat or not, even if they get wet or cold occasionally.
- Understand what pocket money is and how to buy and budget (probably with help).

By the time they are 11 years old most children should be able to:
- cook simple meals
- make a cup of tea or coffee
- vacuum, dust and polish
- be responsible for their own clothes
- manage their own pocket money
- buy simple shopping unaided
- be selective with their TV viewing
- pack their own school bag including knowing when they need PE kit, particular books, etc.
- be responsible for their own time-keeping

Good habits learned early in life are very rarely forgotten. Children with disabilities should be encouraged to become as independent as possible. At least they will know how and will be prepared for the future. A child may quickly revert to being 'spoiled' when they find someone to do things for them.

Busy parents and carers often find it easier to do many of the above tasks for the child, particularly if the child is disabled. However, they should resist the temptation and let the child learn for themselves. Not only will it develop independence skills but will help the child's confidence and self-esteem.

Activity 7: Child's worries checklist

	This is a problem for me at the moment:		
	Yes ✔	Sometimes ✔	Never ✔
Starting playschool			
Starting school			
Going to school			
Changing school			
Going to secondary school			
Family arguments			
Too many arguments			
Grown ups complaining			
Being told off too much			
My brother punching me			
My relatives growing old			
My baby sister			
Brother or sister running away			
Being bullied at school			
Being left out of things or games			
Children always picking on me			
Homework			
Not as clever as I would like to be			
Having to keep secrets			
Friendship problems			
Other children being cruel to me			
Friends may turn against me			
Friendships breaking up			
Making a fool of myself in front of friends			
Having to go to court			
Not sleeping well			

	This is a problem for me at the moment:		
	Yes ✔	Sometimes ✔	Never ✔
Life			
I feel all mixed up about life			
Getting the blame			
Not being trusted			
Telling lies			
Nobody understands me because I'm Asian/ Jewish/Sikh/Hindu/Muslim/ African/ Caribbean			
No one to help me with my troubles			
No one cares			
My body is not well developed			
My height			
I'm too fat			
Not strong enough			
What to wear			
My hair not going right			
My work not being neat enough			
Cruelty to animals			
My pets			
Car accidents			
Being run over			
People taking the Mickey			
Meeting new people			
People my age not liking me			
What people think of me			
People thinking I've done something wrong because I'm 'in care'			
People talking about me behind my back			

	This is a problem for me at the moment:		
	Yes ✔	Sometimes ✔	Never ✔
Noises during the night			
Not having anyone in my class/ neighbourhood/school who looks like me			
My mind going blank at important moments			
Paying bills when I grow up			
Being called names because I'm Asian/ African/Caribbean/Jewish/Sikh/Hindu/ Muslim			
No home when I grow up			
Dying			
Getting fat			
Monsters			
Ghosts			
Having nightmares			
Missing my Mum			
Missing my Dad			
Missing my brothers and sisters			
Missing my pet			
Being bullied all the time			
Hurting myself deliberately			
Being called names because I'm 'in care'			
Being picked on			
Any others?			

Activity 8: Carers' worries

Here is a list of carers' worries. It often helps to know that others have similar worries to your own:

	Effects on my own children and on family life
	Behaviour of children
	Impact on family relationships
	Extended family attitudes and involvement
	Lack of understanding
	Lack of rest
	Lack of specialist help
	Not being happy about plan for the child
	Others don't understand
	No one to talk to
	Social workers don't listen
	Not being able to get hold of social worker in a crisis
	Neighbours
	Masturbation by child
	Child unable to explain worries or difficulties
	Child unable to make any relationships
	Contact with families of origin
	Lack of continuity for children if they go home and the foster carer takes on new children
	Allegations by foster children against them
	Children being moved when they don't agree
	Effect of fostering on own children
	The abuse of other children in the home by those who have been abused themselves
	How to deal with inviting birth family into my home
	How to deal with the child when they are emotional and carer's feelings are raised
	How to help the child at school
	How to help the child in the community
	How to help the child if he or she is being bullied
	How to make the child feel part of the family
	Child disclosing abuse
	How to know what's best
	Conflict between parents and carers on what's best—who decides? Can decision be changed?
	Bedwetting by the child

	Effect on own children—different expectations
	Sexualised behaviour by the child
	The child running away
	The child answering back
	Not having the knowledge and skills to support the child in my care
	Fear of not being able to control the child
	That the child might breach own controls
	The child stealing from neighbours
	Embarrassment
	Complaints from parents
	Children not fitting in
	Children not coping
	Parents not liking you
	The child taking anger out on you
	Doing it right
	Being accepted as substitute mum
	What happens when the child leaves you
	Saying goodbye, making it a happy time
	Keeping tears until after they've gone
	Parents encouraged to complain—we can't complain.

There are sure to be many more that could be added to the list!

Activity 9: Going into hospital quiz

What do these words mean?

Surgery	Medication
Nurse	Anaesthetist
Routine	Doctor
Sister	Surgeon
Porter	Ward
Clinic	Splint
Injection	Operation

What other words can you think of to do with hospitals?

You could look these up in the dictionary or you could write what you think first and then check in the dictionary to see if you are right!

Activity 10: Know yourself checklist

This short questionnaire is something a child could do on their own, with a friend or with their carer.

Write down

3 things you are good at:

1. ....
2. ....
3. ....

3 things you are not so good at:

1. ....
2. ....
3. ....

3 ways you could improve:

1. ....
2. ....
3. ....

3 likes or hates:

	Like			Hate		
in food?	1.	2.	3.	1.	2.	3. ....
in clothes?	1.	2.	3.	1.	2.	3. ....
at school?	1.	2.	3.	1.	2.	3. ....

Other things you like or hate: ....

....

The 3 best points about yourself:

1. ....
2. ....
3. ....

The 3 worst points about yourself:

1. ....
2. ....
3. ....

3 ways you could improve on your worst points:

1. ....
2. ....
3. ....

What do you dislike most about other people? ....

....

If it annoys you to answer these 'stupid' questions, think about why?

When it is finished the child could also ask other people how they would have answered the questions.

Activity 11: Story: Sarah and her pets

Sarah lived on a busy main road in a small town. Her house had a garden at the front and back. There was plenty of room to play and to have pets.

When she was four years old her daddy brought her two guinea pigs and a cage to keep them in. Her daddy fixed a large run at the end of the garden where the guinea pigs could play. Quite soon the guinea pigs mated and the female had two baby guinea pigs.

During the summer, Sarah and her daddy looked after two more guinea pigs whilst their friends were on holiday. Very soon these had mated and Sarah had seven guinea pigs happily playing in the run. She fed them and gave them water each day and they ate the grass.

One day the oldest guinea pig died and Sarah was very sad. Her daddy told her that most humans live until they are about 70 years old. Most guinea pigs only live until they are five years old.

As she grew up, Sarah was very lucky, she had many pets. She looked after rabbits, budgies, canaries and stick insects. When one died she was always very sad and she and her daddy buried each pet in the garden in a special place which Sarah marked with some stones.

When she was ten years old, she was especially happy. She was allowed to have a dog as a pet. This dog she called Toby. It was a very happy, playful, mongrel puppy.

One day whilst Toby was playing in the garden, he jumped over the gate at the side of the house. He ran down the garden path and straight into the road. There was a screech of brakes and a thud.

Everyone ran to the road but sadly, Toby was dead, run over by a car.

The car driver was very upset because he had killed Toby. Sarah's daddy was upset because he hadn't made the gate tall enough to stop Toby jumping over. Sarah was upset because her favourite pet had died. She blamed herself for not being there to stop Toby jumping over the gate.

This is the same when someone we love dies. Everyone blames themselves when really it is no-one's fault.

Section 6: Practical Information

Education

Education is a good way to build a sound future. Education takes place everywhere, in the home, in the street, at school. Children really need your help to get the best from education. A child's education is of the utmost importance. Every effort should be made by all those concerned to:

- get the child back into school as soon as possible but only if they appear ready
- ensure regular attendance
- organise meetings/appointments out of school time
- arrange any extra help a child needs to enable them to catch up or keep up
- ensure they get appropriate teaching support, speech therapy etc. if the child is disabled
- enable any child who is not being taught in an area close to where they are living to join groups or clubs, such as after school clubs, so that they can meet children living in the same area

Children and young people in care are worried that:

- there is a stigma in schools about being looked after
- they are getting behind with their work because of poor attendance. This often makes them not want to go to school, which makes matters worse
- their concentration is not as good as it should be; worries, disturbances or neglect may well be the cause
- they have frequent changes of schools
- the time it takes to get into a school after a move is too long. It is recommended that this should not be more than three days
- they are not getting sufficient extra help to enable them to catch up
- sometimes they are treated differently at school for various reasons, being in care or disabled or because of their skin colour
- if they are disabled they may have problems moving about the building
- they might be being teased
- they are being bullied

Children need help. Children out of school is a national problem and looked after children appear to be particularly vulnerable. Here are some ideas other carers have suggested to help ensure a child is in a school and remains in a school.

1. Make regular visits to the education office to get things speeded up, in order to get a child back into school or being home tutored or anything else that may be needed.
2. Work in partnership with teachers when helping children with their education to avoid confusing the child by using different methods e.g. reading and numeracy techniques.
3. Help them with their weaker subjects, such as reading or spelling.
4. If carers do not feel able to help them with their homework they could find someone else who can; for a black child there may be someone from the same ethnic minority group who could help.
5. Encourage children, praise them, and show you are interested in all they do.
6. If a child is disabled make sure the school has suitable access facilities.
7. If children are being discriminated against or bullied, the school will want to know so appropriate action can be taken. Schools often genuinely do not know about bullying.
8. If going to school seems to be a problem for the child, discuss this with their teacher, head teacher, education welfare officer (sometimes educational social worker) or anyone else who may be able to help to ensure the child achieves their educational potential.

Good habits learned from an early age will hold a child in good stead in later life: **learning is fun; gaining knowledge can be exciting; making the most of one's ability increases self-esteem.**

Getting the best from one's education means that life will be much more enjoyable because skills will be learned to ensure that learning is fun, exciting and makes you feel good. Learning goes on all the time, at home, at school, at play.

Children of all ages need opportunities to learn:
- sounds, music, songs
- about their home and the environment and to help in the home
- about shapes, colours, forms—maths is everywhere
- to draw, paint, construct and grow things
- to handle and manage money
- to read, not just books, but signs, notices and adverts
- to chat and converse with people of all ages

Children need the chance to experience all of these with gradual increases in depth and difficulty. The cost is small; all that is required is the carer's time, thought and effort.
- When you're out together, notice what's going on around you, and talk about it. Why are the people digging up the road? Are all the cars the same?
- Visit the library.
- Go to a park or open space as often as possible, so that the child can practise running, jumping and climbing.
- Teach the child about road safety, and show how it's done by your example.
- Play observation games when in the car such as simple 'I spy' or collecting pub names or car number plates.
- Take a calculator to the supermarket and work out the cost of the shopping.
- Count the change from shops or on the bus.

Carers looking after children who have disabilities will need additional information. Blind children will learn Braille. Schools will provide children with Braille paper but if they need extra this can be purchased from the RNIB.

Visually impaired children may not learn Braille but carers may need to access large print books.

Under 5s

There are many activities carers can do with children which will help them to develop physically, emotionally, socially and mentally. These might be:

Physically

Ensure the child:
- eats a well balanced diet
- has regular sleep
- has plenty of exercise
- has a warm, safe environment with regular mealtimes and bedtimes
- is safe from the risk of physical harm or stress
- lives in an atmosphere that is unpolluted by cigarette smoke

Emotionally and socially

Help the child to experience:
- being with caring adults and other children
- physical closeness and affectionate touching which in no way abuses a child's trust
- routine and flexible caring
- the security of belonging
- a sense of personal identity and self esteem
- feeling valued
- being praised for an achievement
- problems of anger and to learn self-discipline and control

Mentally

Enable children to:
- have a wide range of experiences
- visit, explore and investigate different places, both local and distant
- learn and practise different skills
- set achievable goals
- accept failure as just another of life's experiences
- develop language, communication and motor skills
- learn through play, reading, talking and listening

Play is vitally important for all children. Many children in care may never have played. Learning goes on constantly and reading need not be confined to books. Use the many opportunities around you:
- comics and magazines, television
- shops, signs, advertisements, notices
- instructions on packets or cartons
- recipes
- road signs

Try to create an environment in which learning can occur naturally. It will enhance a child's self esteem.
- Make opportunities for the child to hear about adults' experiences and their lives. Children usually love this.
- Let the child experiment within a safe environment.
- Set targets and goals.
- Join in.
- Above all encourage and praise.

Most children will benefit by joining one of the many pre-school groups that are available. Families from different traditions and cultures may have different expectations of children. Some would say that our 'Western culture' encourages children to grow up too fast. Carers will need to discover any special expectations the child's family may have.

Pre-school establishments vary greatly from area to area. Good sources of local contacts are health visitors, libraries and churches, mosques, temples etc.

For children with special needs your area may be lucky enough to have a 'portage scheme'.

Portage is a home-visiting educational service which helps parents or carers teach their child. The parent or carer plays the most important part in the portage way of working. Portage is aimed at the families of pre-school children whose development appears to be delayed. It is also aimed at parents or carers of babies who had a recognised disability at birth.

Portage offers support to the parents and carers for the children in their area. Health visitors, teachers and medical specialists work with carers and parents often in the home. Unfortunately this scheme is not available in all areas. Ask about it or any other similar schemes from your health visitor, education officer or social worker.

Your health visitor will have lists of local agencies who will be able to help with specific difficulties. The Local Education Authority should also provide neutral advice.
There are agencies that support families in the home. The names vary from region to region such as 'Family Link', 'Home-start'. Some agencies also provide different forms of respite care. Health visitors, social services and early years services should be able to put you in touch with these agencies. They are all free.

Starting school

During my time working as a teacher I had a spell taking the reception class of 28 four to five-year-olds. Very early on in the term, one father told me that Christopher could read. To a limited extent that was true, but many of the life skills he was capable of learning had not been taught.

I believe I spent at least one third of every day performing minor tasks for these children which if they had been taught at home would have made the children happier and more secure and enabled me to spend more time teaching other skills.

Children should be able to do things on the following checklists by the time they start school. Some children with special needs may take longer to learn some of these skills. Children will integrate better if they can master simple tasks and so learn to become more independent.

Practical

Can the children:

- Dress and undress themselves including buttons, belts and shoe laces? (Velcro fasteners are a boon).
- Hang up their clothes?
- Identify their own clothes?
- Recognise and pack their own school bag?
- Recognise and use their own lunch box. It is particularly important that a child's lunch box has some form of permanent identity as many boxes produced look the same.
- Unscrew and tighten their drinks bottle and use knife, fork, spoon correctly?
- Go to the toilet unaided, including redressing? If the child is a boy, can he use a urinal?
- Wash their hands properly, so that when they paint at school they can wash it all off?
- Blow their noses?
- Dispose of rubbish in a bin?
- Use hearing aids or inhalers, or care for their glasses? (Carers should ensure the child wears or brings them to school).
- Say their full name and, as soon as possible, their address?

How can carer's help?

- Practise the above tasks with children regularly before they start school, including showing a boy how to urinate standing up.
- Choose clothes and shoes that are practical, and easy to wear, wash and keep clean.
- Label everything including socks. Show the labels to the child.
- Put a spare pair of pants or knickers in the school bag in case of accidents if you think this might happen. Let the child and teacher know they are there.
- Have PE kit washed and ready for use on the days required.

Emotional and social

Can the child:

- Quickly settle in at new places such as playschool?
- Sit still for five or ten minutes?
- Share and take turns in a game?
- Recognise boundaries at home such as switching off the TV when told or going to bed at suitable bed times?
- Listen, understand and reply?
- Play alone and with others?
- Respect the property of others?
- Respect their own property?
- Respect all people who may be different from themselves in some way, such as girls respecting boys and boys respecting girls as well as those wearing glasses, using wheelchairs or having different coloured skin?
- Recognise that other people's way of doing things may be different from theirs and that this is not necessarily wrong unless it is harmful?

Sometimes a child will need to understand a different language at school from that which is spoken at home (some Asian children speak only their mother-tongue before starting school). Carers need to help the child accordingly, and a specialist teacher must be provided.

How can carers help?

- Give the child a wide variety of new experiences such as train or bus rides, going to the park, feeding the ducks, visiting family or friends.
- Sit with the child and read with them and to them, not just at bedtimes.
- Take the child to the library to get books out.
- Sit with the child when watching TV and talk together about what you have seen.
- If it is possible, take the child to a play scheme, toddlers' club or playgroup.
- Have their friends in to play and have your friends' children in to play so they meet a wide variety of children.
- Take other children on outings with the child.
- Point out that two 'wrongs' don't make a 'right'.
- Explain why other people's property is important. Talk about how upset a child would be if it was their toy which was broken.
- Discuss the difference between right and wrong and the need to tell the truth.
- Compare other people's way of life and ways of doing things.
- Visit different families and locations.

Before a child starts school:

- Take the child to look at the building whilst the other children are out playing.
- Talk about what being at school will be like.
- Many schools organise pre-school visits and part-time schooling for a short time before the child actually starts school.
- Take the child to meet the head and their new form teacher, and explain what is going on and what to expect and why.
- Tell the child why going to school is important.
- Help the child to meet and get to know someone who is already at the school so there will be a familiar face when they first go.
- Give the child some clues about what to say if asked about their family and where they live. Explain about families, foster carers, mums and dads and other carers.

It is important to put the child's name down at the school as early as possible.

When children start school, it's often the noise that frightens them. Tips when leaving the child at school for the first time:
- If the teacher agrees, and the child wants it, leave something familiar, such as a shopping bag, somewhere they can see it at the school.
- Ask the child what they would like to eat when they get back from school.
- Explain that when you leave them you will go to buy their choice of food.
- Talk about what you will do together when they get home.

Carers should give the school the names of people who are allowed to collect the child. It is also important that the child is taken to school and collected punctually. To have someone they know waiting at the school gates before and after school will help a child to feel secure.

When children come home each day from school:
- Have a warm welcoming environment for them.
- Give them a drink and talk about what has happened to them during the day. They may not want to talk about school straight away.
- Tell them what you've done during the day too.
- Teach them to change out of their school clothes.

If children tell you about their worries, ask them what they would like you to do.

> **Don't put pressure on a child to achieve your goals.**

What should carers find out before a child starts school?

- The specific times when visitors are encouraged.
- Details of other agencies who might be involved in the child's welfare, such as speech therapists, health visitors, social services, educational welfare officers and educational psychologists.
- Details of the school governors.
- The school routines and rules.
- What school clothing is required (including PE and sports kit).
- The procedures for informing the school about illness, holidays, and other absences and for collecting the child at the end of the school day.
- The calendar for the school year.
- The curriculum offered and the way the school is organised.
- Activities outside normal school hours.

In this way the carer will be able to provide the child with all the things that they need on a day to day basis. The child can then go to school with confidence and will not have to face avoidable set-backs that may harm progress.

School and education

The UK government has issued guidelines so parents and carers know, in theory, what a child will be taught and should know at a given age. The government also intends that children with special needs should be given an opportunity to attend mainstream school if at all possible. The child may need extra classroom support but this should be provided.

Carers should:

- Support their child in every way, not just when there is a problem.
- Ensure the child gets any additional help they need, especially if they have changed schools several times.
- See the teacher regularly but remember the teacher's time is precious. If you make an appointment, keep to it or telephone to say that you can't.
- Go to open evenings with parents if possible.
- Know what the child's homework is; it's usually recorded in their homework book. Show an interest and help if asked, but the child must become responsible for doing it themselves.
- Have a quiet place available where the child can work.
- Fill in reply slips and return them straight away.
- Show an interest; read to or with the child; talk and discuss; make plans; cultivate good working habits. Help if asked, though the child must become responsible for doing it themselves.
- Talk about the child's education with the parents.

Sometimes children are given a 'label' such as 'autistic' which then means they do not access appropriate education. Such labels should be avoided unless a full and thorough assessment has taken place. The preferred term of many professionals is social communication difficulties.

These children may experience:
- developmental delays
- epileptic seizures
- delayed motor and perceptual development
- behaviour which is difficult to understand
- difficulties with interacting with others

They may lack the language skills to engage in a conversation or they may have the skills but are unable to cope with the conversation process.

The most extreme children may be unable to imitate, play make-believe or pretend play. However, children with some of these difficulties frequently display strengths in some aspect of their visual skills.

In the future many of these children will be able to attend mainstream school because of schemes such as the Pelican Project in Portsmouth where the aim is to promote effective learning in children with autism and related needs.

Carers should **not**:

- Compare the child unfavourably with others of the same age when they are within hearing.
- Encourage fighting back aggressively if another child attacks. If possible, it's better to avoid or ignore the other child.
- Allow late nights beyond normal bed times except for special occasions or at weekends.
- Tell their troubles to the child. Children don't understand, and can't help. It makes them distressed and insecure: and then you'll have another problem such as a child not wanting to leave the carer to go to school.
- Be disappointed, irritated or show anxiety if the child is slow to learn. That will make it even harder for them.

Always help the child to succeed. Nothing succeeds like success, or fails like failure.

Many children, before they start school, will want to learn to write. Other children at school will need help with their writing. If you ask at the school they will give you a sheet showing the recommended way for forming individual letters of the alphabet.

Children out of school

If the child is out of school for any reason:
- The carer must inform the school.
- The school should provide school work for the child to do.
- The carer should ensure this work is done and returned to the school for marking and further work received.
- If the child is suspended then a structured school day should be organised at home. A child should not see it as a chance to do nothing! They should not be allowed to just watch TV or go out unsupervised.

Carers should ensure that a child is out of school as little as possible. This may mean suggesting that planning meetings, reviews or life work take place after school or at weekends. It may also mean that the carer has to personally take the child into the school building to ensure that they actually arrive.

Different types of schools

Mainstream schools

These are attended by children who are developing at the normal pattern and rate for their age.

Children with special educational needs should also attend mainstream schools if possible. Many schools integrate all children in the same schools using classroom assistants where necessary. Where the parents request this every effort must be made to accommodate the child in the school. This is part of the government's inclusion policy.

Some of these children will have a statement (record in Scotland) which sets down the extra support that the school must give that child (see page 98).

Many mainstream schools have units attached to them. These units and the reason a child attends them vary considerably from local education authority to local education authority; you will need to check locally. The reasons for a child attending a unit should be clearly stated.

Sometimes what is best for the child is not available. Make a nuisance of yourself, keep plugging away until you are satisfied that the child is getting the education to which they are entitled. It is very easy to accept what people in authority say. If you are not satisfied, say so.

Recently there were five children at a nursery school who all had language difficulties. One father wrote letters and made telephone calls and his child was given a place at a language centre. The other four children so far have not been offered this provision as their parents or carers have not 'shouted loud enough'. It really is worth sticking out for what you know is best for the child.

What are units?

The children in a unit will have specific difficulties and their needs will be judged to be too great to put the child into a mainstream school even with extra support. The aim is to return the child to mainstream education as soon as possible.

In these units children usually work in smaller groups and have individual programmes which give them the particular extra help they need and for which they might be statemented (recorded).

In some units the children are with the mainstream school whenever possible, e.g. playtimes, mealtimes; possibly in art or drama lessons.

Each unit and school will have a system that is best suited to the particular child's needs.

Examples of units:

Nursery Nurture: for children who need a little extra help to get started, perhaps they may be nervous or shy, or find a mainstream class overwhelming. It is hoped these children will gradually fit more and more into mainstream schooling.

Language Centres: for children who may have disordered behaviour, language problems or delays. In some local education authority areas, children's non-verbal skills will need to be at least age-appropriate. In others, children with a language problem and another problem, e.g. behaviour, may be considered for entry. Again, integration with mainstream schools where possible is encouraged.

Diagnostic units: where children attend so specialists have a chance to watch the children to find out what the problems are and suggest the best ways for helping them.

Other units exist for hearing impaired (deaf) children. Where the requirements set down in a statement (record) cannot be met by support in a mainstream school, there are specialist schools or units which cater for these children. It is hoped that all children can have their needs met locally or by being taxied or bussed to a specialist unit or school. However, if the child does not fit into any of these, then 'out-of-county' provision can be made.

In very severe cases this could involve weekly boarding or even attendance at a non-local authority school, such as those run by the National Autistic Society. In rare cases a child may go to a boarding school for 52 weeks a year. Social services and everyone else concerned would have a case conference before such a step was recommended.

Other schools

There are other types of school a child may attend if they have:
- moderate learning difficulties (MLD)
- physical difficulties (PD)
- severe learning difficulties (SLD)
- profound multiple learning difficulties (PMLD)
- emotional and behavioural difficulties (EBD)

All authorities have different guidelines for attendance at these schools. Please check that you know exactly why the child is attending a particular school and what you can do to help. Find out when the child will attend mainstream school.

Some of these terms may vary from place to place but the over-riding principle is the same.

Managing a change of school

Moving to another home doesn't necessarily mean having to change schools, but sometimes a child may wish to change schools.

Most people change schools around their 11th or 12th birthday anyway, when they change to secondary school. Some children will also change schools at around seven years of age when they go from first to middle or primary school.

If a child has to change schools, how is the new school chosen?

There may not be much choice, depending on the area but if a new school has to be found the carer can go to look round a few schools with the child and talk to the teachers and pupils. Whether a child can go to the chosen school will depend on a place being available.

What will it be like starting a new school?

Some things will be done differently; remember:
- everyone takes time to settle in somewhere new
- tell the child to ask if they are not sure about anything
- encourage them to talk about any problems

Why is education important?
- It helps to nurture, cultivate and bring out the child's good points.
- It will open new doors previously thought impossible to open.
- It will help a child to achieve fulfilment in adulthood.
- It may enable the child to obtain a job that will be satisfying, enriching and financially rewarding.

It is therefore extremely important that a change of schools is managed well.

> **Example**
>
> A famous darts player was interviewed. He said he spent as much time practising his maths as he did throwing darts: 'It's no good being a good dart player if you can't work out what score you need'.

Why don't children want change?

- new teacher
- new lessons
- new buildings and classrooms
- new children
- missing old friends
- being youngest instead of oldest
- afraid of people asking questions
- getting it wrong
- being late
- going to wrong room
- fear of being bullied or belittled
- not making friends
- loss of self esteem or status e.g. prefect

What are the symptoms?

- insecurity
- naughtiness
- dreams, nightmares
- sleeplessness
- restlessness
- endless talking

How can the carer help children cope with change?

- Involve them in discussion from the start.
- Take the child to see the outside of the school early on.
- Meet and talk to children already there.
- Think about how you feel about the change and how it will affect them.
- Make plans so the first days go well.
- Before any visit, talk over with the child what they want to know so that you and they are prepared and can ask questions.
- Ensure any new clothes required fit well and are comfortable.
- Obtain any other requirements listed by the school (social services will help with extra money for this).
- Be sure the children know how to get there and that they are on time.
- Read through and check that any rules or regulations are understood.
- When they come home have a warm welcoming environment.
- Don't ask too many questions but show you are interested. Wait and let them tell you about the day when they are ready.

Education of children with special needs

There are many Acts that cover the education of children with special needs.

There are often local support groups that carers and parents of children with special needs may join.

What are the three main categories covered by legislation?

1. Children who find learning significantly more difficult than the majority of children of their age.
2. Children with a disability (mental, physical or both) that makes it hard for them to make use of ordinary schooling in the local area.
3. Children under five years of age who would fall into either of the above if educational provision were not made whilst they are under five years.

Some key words and phrases

Special Educational Provision: means providing help that is extra or different from what is generally made available in Local Education Authority (LEA) schools.

Local Management of Schools: (LMS) or Local Management of Special Schools (LMSS) means that the money available and the decisions regarding the way education will be provided has been given to the schools and governing body.

It is the duty of every LEA to provide full-time, free education for all children up to the age of 16: from 16 to 19 this duty is transferred to the Further Education Funding Council. It is the parent's or carer's duty to ensure the child attends school. It is also the LEA's duty to ensure that children with statements are educated where possible in mainstream schools. This depends on four conditions:

1. The views of the parents or carers have been taken into account.
2. The child's needs can be met.
3. What is provided will not affect other children.
4. It is an efficient use of the money available.

The LEA also has a duty to ensure that children with less significant difficulties also have their needs met. It is the governing body of schools that are responsible for ensuring that these needs are identified and met. This is done using Individual Education Plans (IEPs). The five stage process is as follows:

1. Identify the problem.
2. Agree the action, activities and resources needed.
3. Decide on parent or carer support.
4. Set targets and timescales.
5. Monitor and review.

Schools must now publish information about policies and state the roles of governors, heads, special educational needs (SEN) co-ordinators and other teachers.

What is a statement of Special Educational Needs ('record' in Scotland)?

A statement (record) is a six part document provided by the LEA that covers:
- the child's personal details
- the child's special educational needs (SEN)
- provision for those with special educational needs
- type and name of school
- non educational needs (usually involving the health authority)
- non educational provision, (e.g. speech therapy)

The following are normally included:
- The development of the child in all ways; physical, linguistic, and social as well as educational.
- Any special weaknesses and gaps which may hamper progress, e.g. problems with memory.
- What improvements are hoped for.
- How these hoped for improvements can be made including any specialised equipment, facilities and extra teaching necessary.

How does a carer know if the child needs an educational statement (record)?

If the child is already in school, the needs will have been picked up by tests and teacher observation. IEPs will also show whether school intervention is enough or if outside provision is needed.

If the child is under five years of age the local health authority must advise if the child has, or is likely to have, special needs. It will probably be the doctor or health visitor who does this.

Developmental checks at the clinic are one way in which a child's needs can be identified and followed up. That is why it is so important for the child to be taken along for the checks (page 114).

Can carers ask for a child to be assessed?

Yes. This is usually requested by the school because of the quality of the child's work and the teacher's reports. However, the carer can make the request independently, but the school will be contacted to prove the need.

If a child is under two years their special needs may be assessed if the parent or social worker asks but carers could suggest it. This may not be a formal assessment. If it is then agreed that specialist provision will be needed, a formal assessment will be carried out.

What happens when a child is assessed for a statement or record?

Teachers, specialists, carers, parents and any other interested parties are invited to give their comments on the child. A child and their parents and carers should attend all the meetings and examinations of the child. When all the reports are received a decision is made as to whether a statement (record) will be issued or not.

If a child is statemented there should be regular reviews. For under fives this could be every six months but for most children reviews are every year. Everybody gets the chance to write comments about progress or changes in need. At age 14 an important review takes place and a transition plan is made which looks to the future in terms of further education needs.

The Department for Education have published two booklets on special needs:
    SEN: A Guide for Parents
    SEN Tribunal: How to Appeal

All parents and carers who have statemented children should receive copies from their local authority. Anyone may ask the education office for copies.

Writing a report for a statemented child

It is a good idea for carers, parents and social workers to write the report together about statementing the child. The following are a few tips:

1. The early years

Do you know what your child was like as a baby? Was everyone happy about progress at the time? When did you first feel things were not right? What happened? Did anyone receive any advice or help and from whom? Were there any significant events or changes that affected the child in these early years?

2. Your child now

Consider their:

- general health
- communication
- learning
- behaviour at school

- physical skill
- outside activities
- playing & learning

- self help
- relationships
- behaviour at home

3. The general views

How does the child compare with others of the same age? What is the child good at? What does the child enjoy doing? What does the child worry about? Is the child aware of difficulties? Is there any other information you would like to give, such as advice or reports from other people?

Money

> *'The way allowances work does not help the children to get a sense of reality.'*
>
> **Carer**

> *'If you don't ask, you don't get it.'*
>
> **Young person**

> *'It ought to be written down the money you're entitled to.'*
>
> **Young person**

It is often said by the children themselves that they are better off being in care. What they really mean is that they seem to get new bikes and money for trips that their friends can't afford. It is therefore important that children learn to manage money.

Children should be involved in decision making on how the money is spent so they can learn to plan for their future.

Older children should know what is available and how it is shared out; it gives them a sense of reality and they can learn to make choices in their day to day lives. Older children should be told what everyone is entitled to and why. It will help them understand why some children seem to get more than others.

Some local authorities give clear guidelines on how money should be allocated and spent. Others leave it to the discretion of foster carers, home managers, social workers and even area managers. The NFCA has produced a useful leaflet entitled *Personal Allowances for Children and Young People in Foster Care* which may be helpful.

Whatever the system, children need to be told about it; to be told what they will get both now and in the future; and they need to be involved in deciding how any special allowances are spent. They may also need your help to get it.

> **Example**
>
> A young man from Birmingham was very upset because his carer had decided, without consulting him, that his special needs allowance should be spent on a personal stereo and tapes of his native language, Punjabi.
>
> He desperately wanted a pair of special trainers similar to those worn by the rest of his basketball team. He gave up playing in the team because he was too embarrassed to wear his own trainers; he flatly refused to listen to the tapes and was very angry and resentful.
>
> The carer, with the best will in the world, was giving 'due consideration' to the child's religious persuasion, racial origin, cultural and linguistic background but not considering the rights and responsibilities of that child.

This is a difficult area as someone will always feel unjustly treated but if money matters are discussed freely then children will know what to expect and when.

Special circumstances for giving extra money should be kept to a minimum; money matters must be seen to be fair.

Managing money, budgeting and saving

Learning how to manage money is important to everyone. Children who are being looked after will need special help in this area as their circumstances may never be quite the same again.

Children need to learn about the reasons and importance of saving money and the different methods available to them.

Almost everyone sometimes gets in a muddle with money so it's important that children understand how difficult budgeting is and that they get plenty of practice in managing their own money.

One idea is to give a child a certain amount of pocket money. Agree how it might be divided, say a third to be for long-term saving, a third for saving for a particular item or event, and the rest to spend as they wish.

It is also worth agreeing with the child exactly what you are prepared to pay for and what you expect the child to finance.

The amount of pocket money a child is given must be reasonable; it's a good idea to check with other families close by. Some children get enormous sums and never learn the value of money.

You could take the child to a bank or building society to open an account. An older child should be able to decide which one will give best value to them. You can then talk about (or work out) interest, different types of accounts, and why a particular Bank or Building Society should be chosen.

With some of their money a child could also buy a small safe deposit box where they could keep their money and any other little treasures they may have. If they kept the key themselves it would be part of the child learning to be responsible and taking decisions that affect them: someone will need to keep the spare key.

The child could also keep a written record of 'ins' and 'outs' so they know about managing money. What is important is that children have experience of handling, managing and saving money from an early age. The budgeting sheets at the end of this section may be helpful.

Sex and sexuality

The Children Acts and Orders guidance state that 'the experience of being cared for should include the sexual education of the young person'. As well as practical advice this must cover the part sexuality plays in developing a sense of identity and the emotional implications of sexual relationships. The guidance also recognises that sexuality *'will be one of the most potent forces affecting any young person in the transition from childhood to adulthood'*.

The Local Government Act 1988 (Section 28) at the time of going to press prohibits local authorities from *'intentionally promoting homosexuality or teaching the acceptability of homosexuality as a pretended family relationship'* in maintained schools.

However, the guidance is limited and does not prevent the provision of information or counselling for young people who are, or who think they may be, lesbian or gay.

Foster carers and agency staff have a specific responsibility to talk to young people around issues of risk associated with sex and sexuality. Broadly, sex and sexuality may be experienced as either:
- pleasurable, being associated with the good things in our lives, or
- problematic, provoking negative feelings.

Foster carers and agencies need a framework for working together with young people and their families on these very subjective and often emotive topics. They should also be suitably trained.

Personal relationships and sex

Television, films and magazines often exploit sexuality in order to increase audience figures. Young people often see sex and sexuality as the only thing that matters if they are to have a successful relationship with someone. It is really important that young people learn about **all** aspects of sexuality and are confident to discuss things openly.

Sex should be a normal and healthy part of our lives. As a child grows up, it is important that they discuss, with someone they trust, issues about personal relationships and sex. It cannot be assumed that children have all the necessary facts they need. (see Section 7 on Facts of Life and Puberty).

If a child asks a question, the carer and child could discuss it or they could look up the information together. Quite often, children as young as eight or nine will hear about things and not fully understand.

Carers must tell parents of any discussions they may have had with the child about sex and relationships so the parents know and are prepared for any questioning.

Things children may want to know about sex and the law

- It is illegal for anyone (male or female) to have sexual intercourse under 16 years of age.
- Rape occurs when a man has sex with a woman without her consent. Rape is a very serious offence. The need for a woman to agree (give her consent) exists because a woman has the right to say 'No'.
- Even when a woman is married, if her husband does not obtain her consent to sexual intercourse, this could be an offence of rape.
- Indecent exposure is where someone commits an act in a public place which is considered obscene, for example if a man exposes his penis or bare buttocks.
- Neither residential carers nor foster carers can have a sexual relationship of any sort with someone for whom they are caring.

When can a girl get pregnant?

A girl can get pregnant the first time she has sex:
- even before her first period
- even if she has a period at the time
- whatever position is used
- even if she only gets semen near her vagina
- without having full intercourse

When a man and woman have sex they risk starting a baby.

What does being lesbian or gay mean?

Children and adults may have feelings for someone of the same sex. This does not automatically make them lesbian (female) or gay (male).

If when they are older it transpires that they are lesbian or gay, then they will need positive and non-judgmental support. There are groups and helplines offering help and support for young lesbians and gays, both nationally and locally.

Can disabled people have sexual relationships?

Disabled children have the same feelings and concerns as non-disabled people. However, they may find it more difficult to deal with these feelings because society often portrays disabled people as non-sexual. Very little information on sexual matters is aimed at disabled people, so it is important they have someone they trust to discuss issues with them.

Staying with friends

During their time being looked after by social services there often seems to be a lot of niggly little rules and regulations that cause discontent amongst children.

Staying with friends is one such set of rules. If you explain the reasons why the rules are there, they may still not like them but at least they will understand.

Can a child go to stay with friends?

Yes, of course, children can but you will need to ask where they are going and who they are going to stay with.

You or the child's social worker will have to find out all you can about the people they want to visit. The parent's or guardian's permission may be necessary. A police check may also have to be made.

Why does this have to happen?

While children are being looked after by social services, you must be sure they are safe and well at all times.

Although asking questions about the people they want to visit may be annoying or embarrassing for the child, it has to be done to ensure the child's safety. It also ensures that there won't be people present that the child is not meant to see.

Life skills

There are some people who would say that it is not right for carers to impose their values and rules on children. But if you talk to young people who have left care or who have started work they may well say that there are certain standards they wish they had learnt. Some of these are:
- Sitting at a table for meal times and having regular meal time rituals such as everyone starting to eat at the same time, serving the food from dishes on the table or asking permission to leave the table when finished eating.
- Laying and using crockery and cutlery correctly, including using a cup and saucer.
- Learning regular habits such as health care, sleeping and exercise.
- Not interrupting or talking whilst others are talking.
- Planning to make good use of time including punctuality.

This can be done by giving a child a watch and diary at quite an early age and ensuring they learn to attend appointments correctly. A child will at first need your help but gradually they can take responsibility for themselves. They should also develop responsible habits such as having the correct equipment or books with them, being reliable and not letting others down.

Children can learn to do this by:
- Being made responsible for packing and taking their own PE kit with them.
- Doing their homework unprompted and with the minimum of help.
- Learning that other people will be disappointed if they let someone down by not turning up or by being late.
- Being encouraged to thank people who have sent them a present or who have been particularly thoughtful to them (if it is appropriate to their culture).
- Being thoughtful, considerate, respectful and kind to others.

Play, hobbies and leisure time

No-one is too old to play. When children are very young their play will be largely dependent on what their carers and teachers provide in the way of resources.

As children get older they will start to develop particular interests which should be nurtured and encouraged. These will help them to develop their own individuality. It will also help them later in life as they become independent.

Play

I was waiting for my niece at a maternity unit in a hospital in Aberdeen. In the corner of the waiting room was a section cordoned off for children to play. Linda's son Michael played happily there for about an hour. The first two or three minutes were spent with cars and a garage but after that he played with dolls. When his granny came along she said *'It's a good job his father can't see him, he'd go mad. He thinks dolls are for girls.'*

Sadly this attitude is reflected everywhere. There are stereotyped ideas as to what girls and boys should do. Teachers will tell you that when children start school or playgroup many boys make a bee-line for the 'Wendy' house to make tea and do the cooking or to the dressing up corner where they don skirts, shoes and hats. All perfectly natural but something they have not experienced before.

Children should be given opportunities for all sorts of play both before they start school and afterwards:

Exploratory: picking up, looking at and later talking about and assembling.

Relational: banging things together, putting one inside the other, then doing puzzles and jigsaws.

Pretend or symbolic: brushing hair, sailing a boat, driving a car. Young children need symbolic play before they can develop language.

Sequenced or imaginative: tea party, making pastry, telling a story.

Role play: dressing up, acting a play, making music.

Expensive toys are not needed for any of the above activities. Try using:

- cardboard boxes
- yoghurt pots
- plastic bottles
- spoons
- sand
- water
- paper, paint
- glue
- string

in fact anything that is readily available. With help they will enable the child to enjoy their play and develop emotionally and socially.

Children need opportunities to play with other children of all ages; to play alone and to 'play' with adults as in helping to mend the car and doing the washing up.

There may be cultural differences and expectations about play. Carers will need to find out all they can and make appropriate opportunities available to the child.

Hobbies and leisure: what to do in freetime

Children will find life more fun if they have interests outside the home. It will:

- Help them build self-confidence, give them a purpose, something to aim for and to achieve.
- Help them make new friends and build a new identity.
- Give them somewhere different to go.

Many children will need a lot of help and encouragement to begin with. Children with disabilities should have the opportunity to take part in social, peer group and sporting activities. Some children may prefer special clubs but many will want to be included in mainstream activities as an equal.

The child likes sport. What can they do?

Many towns have swimming pools, roller-board parks, sports and leisure centres, tennis courts, five-a-side football pitches, etc. The child could use any of these or, when old enough, join a team and play football, basketball, netball, volleyball, etc. There are sports that disabled children can take part in, such as wheelchair basketball, hockey or tennis or they can take part with other able-bodied children if they wish.

The child likes music. What can they do?

Children can learn to play a musical instrument, join a band or orchestra, make a tape of their own and their friends' music, make a rattle or drum from bottle tops, plastic or tin boxes etc.

The child likes art and craft. What can they do?

Children can paint, draw, act, make music, or just listen or watch; join clubs for photography, stamp collecting etc.; go to art galleries or museums; look for leaflets in their local library or go to a local arts centre and talk to the people there.

If a child is black, carers may get information from city councils or the school for example, on multi-racial and multi-cultural events taking place in their own or neighbouring cities/towns.

Can the child join a club?

Children's clubs, brownies and cubs, offer lots of different activities; they're a good way of making new friends and they don't cost very much. The local youth service may be helpful in putting black children in touch with others and in helping disabled children to take part in their chosen activities by advising on access to the various clubs, etc.

The local authority will pay the cost of a child joining a club and also pay for uniforms.

What else is there to do?

- Attend a church, mosque, temple, gurudawara, or synagogue. They will meet many new people and make new like-minded friends and may take part in healthy cultural and religious programmes for children.
- If they don't want to go to a club or take part in sport, there are plenty of other things they can do, such as reading, making their own clothes, cooking or woodworking. Try getting them to learn a new skill.
- There are countryside and environmental projects to take part in.
- It is worth visiting village halls, community schools and community centres to find out what is going on there.
- Try bicycle riding, horse riding or adventure holidays.

To find out more there will be leaflets at the local library, the local arts centre, sports or leisure centre, education office, community offices. The child may feel too shy to join a club. Why not ask a friend to go with them?

The electronic age—TV, computer games and surfing the net

There is a great deal of debate at present about the pros and cons of children watching TV, playing computer games and using the Internet. There is, however, very little absolutely concrete evidence on either side.

What is known is:

- If a child has a tendency to have epileptic fits then TV or computer screens may start them off because of what is known as 'flicker fusion'.
- If you ask children from 6–16 years they will tell you that some computer games make them feel frustrated and even violent.
- Watching violence on TV may also give a child violent feelings or desires to experiment.
- Watching TV, playing computer games or surfing the net means that a child is inactive. They are not talking to other people, getting fresh air, playing with others or getting any exercise.
- A child may have difficulty discerning fact from fiction.
- Some TV programmes billed as for children are totally unsuitable in their use of language and presentation.
- Children may be entertained and contained by noisy, colourful events, but that is all.

Computer games can help a child with number work or reading, will certainly help their hand-eye co-ordination and can give many children a great deal of pleasure.

Watching TV can also be purely pleasurable but can also teach children about current affairs, wildlife, nature and many other interesting topics. It can also fill a need for lonely children as they feel the presenters are their friends.

What can carers do?

- Select very carefully the TV programmes and video games the child should watch or play and help the child to learn to choose wisely.
- Monitor the use of the Internet.
- Never leave a child alone for very long watching TV.
- Sit with them; discuss what you both have seen, and what you both think and feel about what you have seen.
- Agree on the amount of time in a day a child may sit in front of a screen.
- Plan other activities to replace screen watching.
- Encourage the child to play with other children; to run about or enjoy fresh air.
- Censor the videos, computer games or Internet sites that a child has access to. Some people are not always careful and leave unsuitable material lying around.
- Show an interest in the computer games; use them with the child; talk about them. In this way unsuitable material should not be brought into your home.
- Be aware that the child may be under pressure from their peers to play particular computer games or watch particular TV programmes.
- Talk with parents about which TV programmes the child watches.

There is now an accepted psychological disorder called Internet Addiction Disorder (IAD). which relates to young people who become addicted to computer games or cannot stop surfing the net.

Note: *Some internet providers provide control systems as part of their monthly packages. It is also possible to buy programmes which cut out upsetting or inappropriate activities. The most sophisticated, and therefore unfortunately, the most expensive ones, are the best. None of these are totally foolproof so care and monitoring is still necessary to prevent a child accessing inappropriate material.*

Childminding

Childminders provide care in their own homes for children who are not related to them. For example, many childminders look after children before and after school. Other childminders look after babies and young children all day whilst the parents or carers are at work.

Childminders must register with their local authority and will have to comply with very strict rules and standards. For every child who is looked after a contract will be signed by the minder and the parent or carer.

There has been a lot of publicity about the question of whether a child minder may 'smack' a child. This issue needs to be discussed and resolved before a child is left with a child minder.

A list of registered childminders can be obtained from social services offices, libraries, or citizens advice bureaux.

Crèche

Crèches provide safe, supervised group care for children whose parents and carers are involved in an activity on the same site or close by. Crèches may be open all day, but the children only attend sessions on a part-time basis.

If a crèche opens for more than six days a year a very strict code of practice must be followed including registration by the local authority.

Baby-sitting

This is a very difficult area as there are no absolute legal requirements as to age or qualifications. It is recommended that baby-sitters should not be under 16 years.

The Red Cross have started a scheme of teaching basic first aid to baby-sitters. Some colleges also offer courses covering various aspects of child care which may be suitable for baby-sitters.

It is a good idea when choosing baby-sitters to:
- Ensure they know what to do in an emergency.
- Tell them about any special needs the child may have.
- Tell them where you are, what time you will be back and if possible give a telephone number.

The most important thing is that the child is comfortable and happy with the person you have chosen and that you have confidence in and trust that person.

Death of a child whilst in foster care

As a foster carer you will mostly be dealing with children who have been poorly treated or badly cared for in the past. Sadly, because of the backgrounds of many foster children, there is a greater chance of a foster child dying than there is of a non-fostered child dying. Therefore foster carers need to be prepared for this eventuality.

The death of a child or young person always seems to be more tragic than the death of an adult. Whenever a child or young person dies the people closest need support and sympathy from those around them during the grieving process (see p 70).

In the traditional family unit, some consolation can be found in making appropriate funeral arrangements for the deceased. Also those nearest and dearest usually rally round in support. The bereaved can of course immediately return to work to keep themselves busy if they wish. None of this means that they will ever 'get over it'.

Unfortunately, for foster carers, the death of a foster child may be even more traumatic because:
- The law states that upon the death of a fostered child the parents or the local authority are responsible for the funeral arrangements. So, unless you have made some prior arrangements with the agreement of the parents or local authority you could find yourself excluded from making any decisions about the funeral arrangements. You may not even get the chance to attend the funeral.
- Some agencies have no policy for dealing with this situation. It might seem as though foster carers are not expected to have any feelings of grief; that they will just shrug it off and move on to the next placement. The very quality that enabled them to be carers, their ability to care for and give love to the foster child, may seem to be discounted by many agencies at this time.
- Social workers may be reluctant to place another child with the foster carer for a while despite the fact that most people return to work quickly after a bereavement . There is a strange belief that it is best to 'wait a while' before placing another child with the bereaved foster carer, even though the carer may want to take on another child.

If a foster carer has a child with a background that increases the likelihood that the child could die whilst in their care (e.g. a child with HIV, an abused child, a terminally ill child, a drug abusing teenager) there are certain steps that should be taken, in advance, to ensure that, if and when the death occurs, it is managed in the best way possible for all concerned. The foster carer should:
- Ask the agency to explain their policy for dealing with such circumstances. If possible get a written copy of the policy.
- If there is no policy try to get them to tell you how they plan to proceed in your case.
- Try to get them to write formally to you confirming anything you agree.
- Ask the agency to include the arrangements in the care plan for the child.
- Remember that any plans should take into account the following:
    a) Upon death who should be informed and who is to do the informing?
    b) Who is to make the funeral arrangements and are there any religious or cultural issues to be taken into account?
    c) What are the child's wishes, the parents wishes, and brother's or sister's wishes?
    d) Are there previous carers who need to be involved?
    e) What counselling help and support will there be for the foster carers?
    f) Do the police need to be informed?
    g) If the foster carers are not allowed to attend the funeral can an alternative ceremony be arranged?
    h) If there is any media interest (e.g. in the case of a suicide) will there be support from the agency to deal with the media?
    i) Can other children in the house be prepared for the death?

Remember also to agree with the agency that you will most likely be the best person to judge when you are ready to begin fostering again.

Activity 12: Budgeting sheet

Money in	Money out	What's left	Date

Plans for spending in the future ....

....

....

Plans for saving in the future ....

....

....

Section 7: Health

Introduction

This section is based on advice received from senior health officials. For ease of use, the chapters in this section are in alphabetical order.

Good health is not just about the absence of, or presence of, disease. It is about the overall physical, emotional, mental and sexual well-being of the child. As such it is totally linked to the overall development of the child.

All children on entry to care should have an initial health review by their own GP. This is an opportunity to clarify past and present health.

Good health is important because:

- if children get ill or have an accident they will get better quicker
- they will probably get ill less often
- they will have less time off school and will make better progress
- they will be better able to cope with stress and relationships

We have not tried to cover everything in this specialised section but have tried to give a few pointers, hints and suggestions. Health visitors for the under fives, school nurses for the older children and GPs will be pleased to help.

When a child is first looked after a carer may need to know:

- What illnesses has the child had?
- What medication the child is taking—what quantities and at what intervals?
- What injections has the child had?
- Has the child been in contact recently with anyone who is infectious?
- Does the child have any allergies?
- Does the child have any particular health or dietary needs?
- Are there any family illnesses which it is important to know about, such as a heart condition, diabetes or sight problems?
- Does the child have any physical impairment?

In some cases the child may have a particular illness, such as diabetes, and the carer will need specialist advice and training before the child can live in the carer's home.

The above information may be kept on a Health Record Sheet like the one shown on page 149, or on the parent's own record of their child's health.

healthy people

Alcohol

Like tobacco alcohol is a drug. As with all drugs, if it is not used sensibly it can cause problems. Drinking too much alcohol can damage health.

It is important to tell children about the dangers of alcohol, as normally they only see the 'romantic' or 'macho' side of alcohol on television. Equally, it is important to set a good example of safe, enjoyable drinking.

If a child does, either accidentally or deliberately, drink too much alcohol to the point of becoming unconsciousness they risk developing low blood sugar levels and should be taken to hospital as a precaution.

Allergic illnesses

Allergy is an abnormal reaction by the body to substances, often harmless, which are breathed in, swallowed, injected or come into contact with the skin. Allergy to food seems to be on the increase with the use of additives in food.

Allergies should be diagnosed with caution under medically controlled conditions. Children need a balanced diet. Removal of foodstuffs from a child's diet on shaky evidence of allergy can do more harm than good.

Asthma is by far the most common chronic illness in childhood affecting one in seven children in the UK. Spasm of the small tubes in the lungs makes it difficult to breathe. It shows itself by irregular bouts of coughing, sneezing and breathlessness.

Asthma attacks are usually brought on by contact with pollens, feathers, fur (furry pets like dogs, cats, rabbits and hamsters) house dust and house mites. A major trigger for an attack is cigarette smoke. Allergy to food is a less common cause. Other factors may be chest infections and colds, vigorous exercise, emotional upsets, stress, sudden changes in temperature and, on rare occasions, laughter.

Nowadays, treatment for asthma is very good and most children are able to lead a normal life and attend school regularly. If children cough at night, wheeze or cannot fully participate in sport they are not being treated correctly and should visit a GP or hospital asthma clinic. The aim of treatment is to be *symptom free*. It is most important that preventative inhalers (often inhaled steroid) are taken regularly and consistently. Don't make the mistake of stopping them because the symptoms have gone away. A child should only stop taking medication on medical advice.

Eczema affects the skin. The key to treatment is to keep the skin moist with regular emollients (greasy creams, bath oils, ointment) and treat flare up with steroids or antibiotics as directed by your GP.

Hay fever causes sneezing and running eyes and nose. Children allergic to tree pollens (e.g. Silver Birch) tend to wheeze in spring. Those allergic to grass are affected in the summer.

Many of these conditions may appear worse in times of stress.

Dental care

Teeth can last a lifetime if they are looked after well.

Dental care should begin as soon as teeth appear. The age at which a baby can have the first tooth coming through can vary from birth to 18 months or so. In most babies they begin to appear from about the age of six months and usually all the baby teeth are through by about the age of 2¹/2 years. There are 20 baby teeth altogether and the lower middle teeth usually come first.

- Teething does not cause illness, although it may cause discomfort.
- Tooth decay is avoidable.
- Restrict sugar-rich foods and drinks to mealtimes.
- If a child is thirsty between meals, give water or very dilute unsweetened fresh fruit juice.
- If a dinky feeder is used put only plain water in it.
- Don't give baby a bottle to suck to go to sleep.
- If it is necessary for the child to take medicine ask your doctor or chemist for a 'sugar free' one. If not available, a child's teeth and gums should be cleaned after taking medicine.
- Clean teeth thoroughly at least once a day using a fluoride formulation.
- As soon as baby's first tooth appears, clean with a very small, soft toothbrush.
- Always brush teeth before going to bed.

Children need help to brush their teeth properly until they are about seven years old. One method is for the carer to stand behind the child and gently tilt the head upwards so that all tooth surfaces can be brushed using a scrubbing movement.

Fluoride makes teeth strong. Use a blob of fluoride toothpaste about the size of a pea. Ask your dentist or health visitor about fluoride supplements.

Regular dental checks

Introduce the child to a dentist early on, before trouble starts. Get into the habit of regular check-ups, so that the dentist can check the teeth and help to prevent any decay.

Developmental assessments and health assessments

Taking the child to see a doctor

The child should ideally be cared for by the family's own GP as they will know the family background. If this is not possible the carer's GP may see the child with the agreement of the child's parents as they will usually still have parental responsibility.

Try to get the parents involved with any non-emergency visits to the doctor and also let them know of any illness the child may have. Parents should delegate responsibility to foster carers for certain medical care particularly for emergency treatment. The social worker should have the information regarding delegated responsibility.

Statutory health assessments

Every child looked after by a local authority should have a medical examination before placement. Arrangements for medicals are changing in some areas. The carer should attend these medicals with the child. If it is possible the parents should come too as they will be the best people to know about the child's background. Ideally the family GP should undertake at least the first medical examination.

Some children may prefer to be examined by a doctor of their own sex. This is particularly important if the child has been abused or is from an ethnic minority group.

Note: *The child is allowed to refuse any part of the assessment. Children aged five and upwards should positively give their consent.*

A child who has been abused may be very worried about having a medical examination and will need re-assurance and help to overcome these fears.

Health Assessments must be offered at least once every six months before the child's second birthday and at least once a year afterwards.

Recommended developmental reviews

District Health Authorities have their own schemes of health and developmental checks. They are usually done by the family doctor and the health visitor. Young children should be seen at 6–8 weeks; 6–9 months; 18–24 months and then at 36–48 months. Sometimes the regular developmental review is included when the child has a statutory medical examination. Carers should check that this is the case.

It is very important not to miss developmental checks as these are where health problems such as dislocated hips, vision and hearing impairment, and speech, language and learning difficulties are first noticed. Prompt and early treatment is essential to prevent problems later on in the child's life.

Milestones

Babies develop according to a recognised pattern. 'Milestones' are the ages at which a child first smiles, sits, crawls, walks, etc. There is often wide variation between children; some individuals may be much more advanced in one area of development than another (e.g. the active child that walks early but talks late).

It is time to worry if the child is:
- squinting (lazy eye) after four months
- not sitting by eight months
- not walking by 18 months
- not speaking by two years

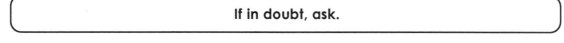

If in doubt, ask.

It is a good idea to keep a record of when milestones are reached. The sheet at the end of the Health Section may be used. This information may be very helpful when assessing a child's development. It is also of interest to the child as they grow up and may be included in the life story book.

Diet

This doesn't just mean losing weight. It means thinking about what children eat, how much they eat and why they need certain foods. The connection between diet and health is now well recognised.

Some healthy foods are:

- fresh fruit
- white meat
- wholemeal bread
- unsaturated margarine
- pasta
- vegetables
- fish

Low fat milk is healthy if the child is over five years old. Children 2–5 years may have semi-skimmed milk if they are thriving well. Under twos should have full fat milk at all times as this contains essential vitamins and calories.

Some foods that can be unhealthy are:

- crisps
- fizzy drinks
- cakes
- sweets
- chocolate

It's not as bad as it sounds. The 'unhealthy' foods are not of course forbidden, but it is a good idea to:

- Cut down on the amount of these a child eats and drinks.
- Grill food instead of frying it.
- Reduce the amount of sugar and salt eaten.

If a child is, or wishes to become, a vegetarian, care has to be taken to ensure a balanced diet. The Vegetarian Society or your GP will give details.

Children from ethnic minorities may have special dietary requirements. The carer may need help to ensure their needs are met.

Problems with food

Some children will not eat very much or pick and choose. Others may want to eat too much. The important thing is not to put pressure on the child or to appear anxious. Try to find ways of getting a child to eat well and healthily; your health visitor or school nurse will be able to give you further help. Children who have been emotionally abused or neglected or have suffered punitive treatment around mealtimes, or even been denied food, may need to learn that eating is safe and enjoyable. See also p 119 on eating disorders.

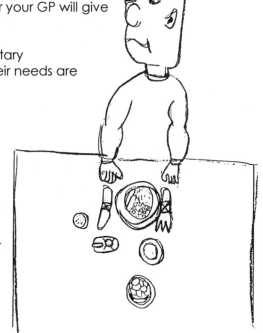

Drug and substance abuse

Many young people will have experimented with drugs in some form before they leave school.

Solvent abuse

After smoking and alcohol 'glue sniffing' as it is commonly called, is the most common form of teenage experimentation. Children often start as young as eight or nine years old but the peak age is thirteen or fourteen years. Most children only do it a few times and then stop. Sadly some do not. They might sniff:

- butane gas (cigarette lighter fuel)
- aerosol sprays
- correcting fluids (Tipp-Ex)
- solvent-based glues (Evo-Stik)
- dry-cleaning fluids
- the contents of some fire extinguishers
- thinners
- petrol
- liquid shoe polish

What to look for

There are no clear-cut signs and many of the effects are hard to distinguish from normal growing up. Moodiness may be a result of sniffing but many children are moody without having tried solvents.

Look out for:

- finding quantities of empty butane, aerosol or glue cans, or plastic bags in a place where you know children have been
- chemical smell on clothes or breath
- 'drunken' behaviour
- sudden change in behaviour or lifestyle, for example, going around with a new set of friends
- wide swings in mood or behaviour
- spots around nose and mouth (glue sniffers rash only occurs with some glues and may not be as common as acne!)
- loss of appetite
- asking for money from their friends or carers without explaining what it is for or with feeble explanations
- secretiveness about leisure-time activities
- frequent and persistent headaches, sore throat or runny nose; a quick visit to the doctor would be useful

> **Don't jump to conclusions but be alert to the signs.**

A young person told us:

> *'Solvent abuse is dangerous because the initial 'buzz' only lasts seconds and continual use is needed to keep the high going (which can lead to suffocation)'.*

Most children under 11 do not experiment with drugs or solvents but the topic may be something a carer would want to discuss with a child, especially if they ask questions.

Why do they do it ?

- It's an alternative to alcohol.
- They like the excitement, the element of danger.
- If adults are shocked, that can be an attraction.
- They like experimenting with new sensations.
- Hallucinations or new sensations can be interesting and exciting.
- Hallucinations can also be dangerous, unpleasant and frightening, but even this can be enjoyable (think of horror films).
- Drugs allow young people to escape—if only temporarily and only in their imagination.
- They may be lonely, feel inadequate, lack self-esteem or confidence and think drug taking will help.
- They think it will help them blot out problems.
- They are encouraged by their friends or made to look small if they refuse.

What drugs are there?

- solvents
- heroin
- sedatives
- ecstasy
- cannabis
- tranquillisers
- crack
- stimulants
- cocaine
- anabolic steroids

The drugs have 'street' names which may change with fashion. Your local drugs advisory service will give you a leaflet showing the latest names.

Many young people will try taking drugs and stop immediately. Sadly others will not. If they start injecting drugs this can be the most dangerous because of the risks of:
- infection where injecting equipment is unsterile and shared. The most serious infections are HIV (which can develop into AIDS) and hepatitis. If a young person is injecting drugs they may get hepatitis B or C. Make sure children know the dangers
- abscesses and thrombosis and other conditions from injecting drugs that were never intended for injection
- gangrene from hitting an artery instead of a vein
- blood poisoning caused by a wound becoming infected
- overdose when a drug of unknown strength is delivered directly into the bloodstream

What should you do if someone is 'high' on drugs?

- Keep calm and patient: you have to try to bring them down.
- Talk to them about how they feel at the moment.
- Ask them questions about where they are or what they can see: pink elephants?
- Gradually, slowly, quietly explain where they are, who you are.
- Keep talking, don't threaten, be pleasant; the time, if appropriate, for punishments and explanations may be later.
- Sometimes the best solution is just leaving them to themselves but you will need to stay alert.

What should you do in an emergency?

- Make sure they've got fresh air.
- Turn them on their side so they won't choke on their vomit.
- Don't leave them alone.
- Get someone to dial 999 and ask for an ambulance.
- Collect any powders, tablets or anything else that may have been used and give it all to the ambulance driver.

How can a carer help prevent drug and solvent abuse?

- Talk to the children and young people about their views on drugs.
- Help them have new, interesting and challenging experiences.
- Get them to think about how they might refuse drugs without losing their friends.
- Teach them to care for and value their health.
- Help them build up their self esteem and respect for themselves.
- Treat them with respect.
- Take an interest in their opinions and worries.
- Check out any problems they may have.
- Arrange other activities and help the child take part in them.
- Seek support from your local drugs advisory centre.
- Be a good listener.

Where can a carer get advice?

At the back of this book there is a list of telephone numbers and addresses of places that may be able to offer advice or help.

Eating disorders

Some very young children have a physical eating condition which they may have had since birth. Other children may develop an emotional eating disorder.

> 'My brother tries to be perfect in every way. He worries all the time about what other people think of him.'

> 'My friend sometimes starts eating and just can't stop.'

> 'My sister has become very distant from us. She seems to keep herself away from us.'

Some of the above signs might mean that someone has an emotional eating disorder. People with an eating problem may eat too much, or refuse to eat, because they are unhappy. This can lead to emotional and physical problems. People often think that eating disorders are just about food and weight, but they are not. They are about feelings as well. People often don't think that children might have this illness.

Eating disorders are a way of coping with feelings that are causing unhappiness or depression. It may be difficult to face up to, and talk about, feelings like anger, sadness, guilt, loss or fear. The eating disorder is an unconscious attempt to avoid these feelings, or keep them under control. It is a sign that the child needs help in coping with life and shows how they see themselves as a person.

There are many reasons why people develop eating disorders. Often there is no one cause, but a series of events that makes the child unable to cope. Examples are:

- changes in the family
- the death of someone special
- problems at school e.g. exams or being bullied
- lack of confidence e.g. moving towards adolescence
- emotional or sexual abuse

If carers think the child has a particular problem with eating they should seek advice. It may be there is quite a simple reason that can easily be put right or the child may need specialist help.

Exercise

It is well recognised that today's children are less fit than in the past. This is due to a changed lifestyle. Regular exercise is essential for everyone. It can be running, jumping, bike riding, swimming or any other type of exercise the child enjoys.

It is strongly recommended that children walk everywhere rather than being taken round in a 'buggy' or car because it is quicker.

Simply walking to and from school or playgroup can be good for everyone. The time can also be spent talking to the child.

Eye care

'Lazy eye' and 'squint' are two very important conditions. A child can become blind in a 'lazy' or 'squinting' eye if it is not treated early. Treatment varies, but may include eye exercises, patching the good eye to make the lazy one work, a simple operation or wearing glasses. Seek an urgent opinion if you see a child over four months old squinting.

Children's eyes should be checked before they are one year old if it is known that there is a family history of sight problems. At school children's eyes are routinely checked on entry to school and once again at the move to senior school.

> **Regular eye tests are essential.**

Facts of life and puberty

Children who are looked after may have changed schools or been off school for sometime so may well have missed out on sex education lessons. It may also be that because of their family circumstances they will not have been told about such matters at home.

It is therefore essential that carers give help and guidance, otherwise a child's only knowledge will have been gained from the playground.

In addition to explaining the biological facts, the carer, when explaining things to a child at an early age, should consider issues of:

- morals
- the law
- relationships
- love
- culture
- respect
- caring
- ethics
- genuine affection
- responsibility towards themselves and others
- sexuality

Different families and cultures will have their own standards and rules about sex. For some, sex and the workings of the body are very private and discussion is taboo. Sometimes children who have been told *'It's wrong to touch, kiss or to talk about sex'* become confused.

Other families and cultures will prefer a more open approach seeing sex as part of normal life. However, when openness becomes permissiveness, problems occur.

Some children may need extra help to understand about the meaning of relationships. Children who have been sexually abused will need particular help to understand and accept any form of sex education. In fact a child may disclose that they have been sexually abused during such a discussion. Carers should always ask for professional help if this occurs.

Different words may also have different meanings to different families. It will help if carers can find out what a child knows or what words were used by their family or previous carer before the child is looked after.

Children need to know about life cycles, reproduction and puberty and to understand about the changes that take place to their bodies. They also need to know about the gradual lead-up to these changes.

If the child does ask questions, the carer needs to be prepared, and to be honest, frank and truthful in their answers. The Family Planning Association have very good leaflets available which also answer many of the questions a child may ask.

The carer may have to tell the child several times about the facts of life etc. as the child may forget or may not fully understand the first time.

It is a good idea to find out from the school at what age sex education begins and what it covers. This area is one where the schools do have a lot of discretion.

If the child has missed the sex education lessons at school and the carer is going to explain things to the child, then the carer should tell the school so the teachers understand if the child starts asking questions about sex.

> **Always advise parents when the child is receiving sex education.
> If possible, invite parents to be present at any discussion or explanation
> that takes place. This will help parents to recognise a child's new needs.**

Using the LAC (see p 164) forms may be an opportunity for open discussion

- Finding the right opportunity to talk to the child is very important. If a child starts making sexual innuendoes or masturbating then this could lead into a discussion on sex.
- If the child starts asking questions relating to sex or reproduction this is obviously a natural way to begin. Whenever you decide the time is right privacy and confidentiality are essential.
- Using the right words is also important. Some children get very embarrassed if very explicit words or pictures are used.

A child may be very naive or very knowledgeable or think they are knowledgeable. Whatever the case, the carer needs to be well prepared beforehand. They should also be willing to say *'I don't know but let's find out'* if necessary.

A head teacher told me that despite an apparent broadening of attitudes, boys still giggle and seem to find sex lessons more difficult to handle than girls of a similar age.

Religion, Ethnicity Sex Education: Exploring the Issues by Thomson is a very good book on the subject of different attitudes to sex and puberty. The following very briefly summarises different attitudes towards puberty:

Hindu girls change their dress to fully cover the body with the onset of puberty. Nothing marks puberty for a boy so one day they just grow up! Information and education is very ad hoc.

Islamic religious duties become strictly obligatory when a child attains the age of puberty. A boy or girl has the option to accept or reject an arranged marriage when they reach puberty.

Jews treat puberty with no special significance. It is seen as a natural stage in the body's maturity.

Sikhs baptise children when they reach puberty. Girls are also treated more protectively. Menstruation is known as an unclean phase and during this time a girl does not take part in religious ceremonies. After menstruation a bath is taken and then a girl returns to normal life.

There is much misunderstanding about the whole question of sex and puberty. What is important is that the children in your care feel able to tell you and to discuss such matters openly, frankly and without embarrassment.

Foot care

Shoes or slippers are not needed until a baby starts to walk.

It is important to make sure that there is always plenty of room for the child's toes in the shoes and socks otherwise the toes may be bent and permanently damaged. 'Babygrows' are very useful items of clothing but can be harmful to a child's feet if they are too small. It is easy to cut off the feet of the babygrow as soon as they start to pull.

Children's shoes should be checked for size every 3–6 months. Their feet should be measured by an approved specialist in a shoe shop. Many people hate trainers and think they are bad for a child's feet, particularly if they are made from synthetic materials. This may be true but a well-fitting trainer is better than an ill-fitting shoe. What is important is that:
- the child's socks fit well
- the child's feet are measured regularly
- the correct size shoes are worn
- the shoes support the feet properly

Growth and development

It is very important to keep a close watch on the growth rate of children. Most children grow at a regular rate. This may not happen if the child has been ill, inadequately fed or continually abused or neglected.

Some children may also put on too much weight or lose weight when unhappy or if they are given an unsuitable diet. This will affect their self-esteem and health in adulthood.

A record of a child's weight and height may be kept by the health visitor, family doctor or school nurse. It is also a good idea for carers to measure the children and to keep a record.

Make sure the height measure is in the same place each time and the child is wearing similar amounts of clothes.

It could become a fun thing to do together and you and the child will see their progress if you record it on the Milestones record sheet (p 148) or on the measuring chart itself if there is room.

Health records

It is a good idea to keep a separate record of a child's health care because:
- Later in life people are often asked to fill in forms about their medical records and it will help them to remember details.
- A child can take the records if they move somewhere else.
- There may be a pattern of regular illness. By looking at their records and thinking what they have done it may be possible to work out why.

BAAF publish a *Carer's Held Health Record a Passport for Health*.

Carers must keep a record of any medicines the child has taken or must take.

In most districts parents of pre-school children are now given responsibility for keeping a child's Heath Record. Soon this is to be extended to school age children. Carers should be given these records or ask for them. Unfortunately, they are often not available or if they are the records are not up-to-date.

Hearing

Young children often have continually runny noses and catarrh, especially about the time that they start at school. The catarrh can block the passages leading to the middle ears. Lympitoid tissue at the back of the throat (tonsils and adenoids) get bigger up to age five years and can contribute to middle ear problems. If this happens, the child's hearing may sometimes be affected.

In younger children a hearing problem may lead to delayed speech and language development. It may also cause listening or attention difficulties all of which may persist in later life.

Poor hearing makes it difficult for a child to understand the teacher in class which may lead to behaviour or learning difficulties. Other children may also ignore them. The hearing of children suffering from glue ear is intermittently affected so repeated testing is necessary.

You may be able to spot a hearing problem if the child:
- turns up the volume on the television
- shouts rather than speaks
- doesn't come when called (if not facing you)
- doesn't form words correctly
- behaves very boisterously or disruptively

Research has shown that having a walkman or personal stereo in the ear for more than an hour a day will cause hearing loss which cannot be put right later. Loud music can also affect hearing. It essential that children do not listen to a walkman for long periods especially at high volume.

HIV or AIDS

HIV is a virus that can get into the blood and destroy the white blood cells leaving the body open to attack from other infections.

AIDS is a condition which develops when the body's defences are not working properly. This means people are more likely to get illnesses which the body would normally be able to fight off easily. These illnesses can be serious or fatal.

At the moment there is no treatment which can cure AIDS.

How is the HIV virus passed on?

- Through intimate unprotected (that is, without condom) sexual contact or intercourse between any two people if one of them has the virus.
- By getting infected blood into the bloodstream when using unsterilised needles or syringes which have been used by an infected person. Drug abusers are especially at risk.
- Via a child who may be infected: carers must be given all necessary information about this.
- Occasionally women who have the virus can pass it on to their babies during pregnancy, at birth or through breast milk.

All donated blood used in hospitals is now tested before it is used and blood products are heat treated to reduce the risk of infection.

You cannot catch the virus by touching objects used by an infected person or by touching an infected person.

Children will have heard a lot about HIV and AIDS and will often be scared because of what they have heard.

If a child is HIV positive, they will need extra help and support as well as education on just what it all means and how it will affect them. Your social worker will make arrangements for this.

Sometimes a child will be HIV positive without anyone realising. Care should always be taken when dealing with blood and giving resuscitation. Carers may get advice from a first aid course or book. If you do a first aid course organised by the British Red Cross Association you will get a copy of their excellent book *First Aid for Children Fast: For Parents and Carers*.

Illness

To protect children from illness, there are some simple measures that can be taken:
- Try to keep children away from people's coughs, sneezes and other infections.
- Ask people not to smoke in the car or in the same house as the child. Breathing in cigarette smoke can damage the child's lungs at any age and cause other serious future problems such as glue ear and asthma, as well as considerably increasing the risk of cot deaths.
- Babies should be kept in a room at an even temperature of about 19 degrees C (65 degrees F). Protect the baby from draughts and from getting too hot.
- Avoid 'over the counter' medicines. They are seldom needed. If a child is ill the doctor will prescribe appropriate medicines.
- Take the child to be immunised.
- Do not delay asking for advice if you think a child is ill. Remember early advice could prevent the child being more ill later.

Knowing when a child is ill

Sometimes there is no doubt, but often it is difficult to tell whether a child is ill. This is especially true when dealing with a young child or a child with 'special needs' as they are unable to communicate their needs.

Immediate help is needed from your doctor if the child:
- has a fit or convulsion
- feels unusually hot or cold or floppy
- is repeatedly sick
- has frequent diarrhoea
- is exceptionally hard to wake, is unusually drowsy or does not seem to know you
- has quick, difficult or grunting breathing
- cries in an unusual way, or for a long period if an infant
- has a hoarse or raspy cough
- refuses food repeatedly, especially if the child is unusually quiet
- has a rash that doesn't disappear with the 'glass test' (this is where you press a glass or bottle against the rash causing the rash to 'disappear' for a while)

Using medicines

Aspirin should not be given to children under the age of 12 years, as it has been linked with a rare but dangerous disease. Child strength Paracetamol in childproof containers should be used instead. All medicines should be kept in a locked cupboard with childproof locks.

Health problems and school

If children are unwell do not send them to school. The school should have a list showing the suggested time a child should stay away from school for common illnesses. For diarrhoea or sickness the child should have been eating normally and have been completely clear for 24 hours before returning to school. For example, if a child is sick or has diarrhoea on Monday, eats and is completely normal on Tuesday, they may return to school on Wednesday at the earliest. Not only do illnesses spread around the school very quickly but the child is open to other infections if they are still unwell.

If a child needs regular medication or medication on an 'as and when' basis, make sure that you have two of everything, one at home and one at school.

Infectious illnesses

Rashes look different on different people. The colour of spots can vary, and on a black skin, rashes may be less easy to see. If in doubt check with your doctor.

Immunisations

It is easy to protect most children against infection with a simple course of injections, but every year children die unnecessarily from dangerous diseases.

Some children require a neo-natal BCG injection. The result of this will be read at the six week health check.

'At risk' children may have missed all or some immunisations. It is most important that these are completed. A course of three Hepatitis injections is available for at risk children.

The suggested ages for the injections are:

Age	Immunisation
2 months	1st Hib injection, 1st Diphtheria, Whooping Cough, Tetanus injection, 1st Polio Drops
3 months	2nd Hib injection, 2nd Diphtheria, Whooping Cough, Tetanus injection, 2nd Polio Drops
4 months	3rd Hib injection, 3rd Diphtheria, Whooping Cough, Tetanus injection, 3rd Polio Drops
15 months	Measles, Mumps and Rubella injection
4 years	Booster Diphtheria, Tetanus injection, Booster Polio Drops, Booster measles and Rubella

Masturbation

Children commonly masturbate as a sign of anxiety or plain boredom. Usually this occurs in under threes. If a child is seen to masturbate, it does not automatically mean that they have been subjected to abuse.

Masturbation may be a soothing and pleasurable human activity. Help the child to understand that it is a private activity. Carers may need to ask for advice.

Overactive children

Many parents say their children are 'hyperactive'. In fact real hyperactivity is rare. But quite a lot of children are extremely active, restless and difficult to manage. And an overactive child, or even a 'normally' active child, will be much harder to handle if, for example, you live in a small flat.

Keep to a daily routine as much as you can. Routine can be important for restless, difficult children. Routine may also help you stay calmer and stand up better to the strain.

Make giving the child some time and attention a part of your routine. In different ways, the child may be demanding your attention most of the day, if not most of the night as well. A lot of the time you will have to say 'No'. This is easier to say, and may be easier for the child to accept, if there are certain times each day when you do give all your attention to the child.

It's often no good even expecting an overactive, difficult child to sit still at meals or behave well in a supermarket. Avoid difficult situations as much as you can, by keeping shopping trips short, for example. Try lowering your expectations. Start by asking the child to be still, or controlled, or to concentrate, for very short times. Make a game of it. Then gradually build up. Try to get out every day you can to a place where the child can run around and really let go. Go to a park, or a playground, or whatever safe, open space there is. Find ways of helping your child burn off energy.

Periods

Many young girls will start their periods at ten or eleven years of age, others will start much later. Whenever it is, they need to be prepared, both physically and mentally. They need to know about:

- Sanitary towels and tampons—they should always have a packet stored in their bedroom so they are ready for the start of their periods.
- Period pains.
- Vaginal discharge that starts sometime before their periods begin.
- The many bodily changes that will be occurring at that time.

There are many myths and different beliefs surrounding puberty both from a cultural and religious point of view. The Commission for Racial Equality has specialists who can advise you if you need further information.

> **Help them to look forward to this new phase in their life.**

Personal hygiene

Make sure children know about the need to wash thoroughly. They should also wash their hands after using the toilet. Changing into clean clothes regularly is essential. Children also need to be told of the consequences if they don't! With the changes that take place in both boys and girls during puberty it is particularly important that personal hygiene is stressed.

Premature (pre-term) babies

Premature babies are smaller than babies born at the right time, but they should grow at a regular rate. They also tend to be later reaching developmental milestones. If a baby is born two months early, it is normal for it to be two months later than the expected time in sitting up and walking, etc. After age two no allowance should be necessary: the child should have caught up.

No allowance should be made for prematurity in the timing of immunisations.

Solid foods should be introduced into the diet when the baby is ready for them.

Some babies born full term are very small and may be late reaching developmental milestones (Mary Sheridan, *Development Lines*—for one view of pre-term babies).

Preventative medicine

The Government has set up Health Promotion Units. The aim is to educate and empower everyone to take control of their lives. The staff give advice on many of the areas mentioned in this section. Health Promotion staff are happy to talk to anyone; will give lectures; mount displays or provide leaflets. Two of their immediate targets are to reduce accidents to children and to encourage everyone to give up smoking.

Resuscitation

Emergency Action

It is strongly recommended that all carers should undertake a first aid course and attend regular up-dates.

Call for medical help but in the meantime:

1. If the child is not breathing:
   a) Check child's response.
   b) Gently shake the child and shout 'wake up'.
   c) Open the airway.
   d) Place the child on its back on a table or other firm surface.
   e) Place hand on the forehead and the other under the chin.
   f) Gently tilt head back.
   g) Look in the mouth and remove any vomit etc.
   h) Check breathing.
   i) Watch chest to see if it rises and falls.
   j) Feel for exhaled air from the child's mouth or nose.
   k) Look at skin colour—is it very pale, grey, or blue?

2. If child remains unconscious and not breathing, shout for help.

3. If you feel there is no alternative and help has not arrived, it may be necessary to start artificial ventilation.
   a) Seal your lips around the child's mouth and nose.
   b) Blow gently into the lungs until the chest starts to rise.
   c) As the chest rises stop blowing and allow the chest to fall.
   d) Repeat this twice.
   e) Check pulse by pressing your fingertips lightly towards the bone of the wrist or on the artery on the neck just to the side of the Adam's apple. For babies whose necks are short and plump, the pulse found on the inner side of the upper arm is easier to feel.

4. If you do not feel a pulse start chest compressions.
   a) Locate a position one finger's breadth below a line joining the child's nipples in the centre of the breastbone.
   b) Slide one hand under child for support. With two fingers for a baby or with the heel of your hand for an older child, press on the chest five times to a depth of 1/2 to 1 inch (2–3 centimetres).
   c) Do this as rapidly as possible. After each fifth compression, blow into the lungs once.
   d) Continue, checking the pulse after a minute and then every three minutes until the child responds or qualified medical help takes over.

5. If you do feel a pulse continue to breathe for the child and check the pulse frequently.

6. When the child starts breathing:
   a) Watch the breathing.
   b) Check the pulse until medical help arrives.
   c) Don't leave a child lying on its back if breathing, put child in the recovery position on their side—shown here.
   d) Ensure airway is kept open.

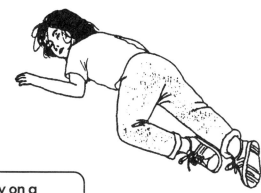

> **Never practice on a healthy infant; only on a mannequin or doll.**

For a fit or convulsion

1. Lay the child on its tummy with its face turned to the side and its knee up on the same side.
2. If child is hot, loosen or remove clothing and cool the head and body by sponging with lukewarm water (don't use cold water).
3. Don't try to put anything in the child's mouth: you may damage their teeth and you might get bitten.

Most fits in non-epileptic children are due to a fever, usually called 'febrile convulsions'. They are usually brief and stop without assistance. After a fit the child may be drowsy for a while. Children prone to febrile fits should be given paracetamol or ibuprofen syrup whenever they develop a fever.

For a burn or scald

1. Douse the burn or scalded part liberally in clean, cold water, preferably under a running tap for five minutes.
2. Do not try to remove clothing.
3. Do not apply any cream, oil or ointment.
4. Lightly cover part with clean pillow case, sheet or cloth.

For an accident

1. Give first aid if you know how.
2. Get the child to hospital.
3. If the child has swallowed pills, medicines or household liquids, take the container to hospital with you.

It is important to have a first aid book in the house.

Safety and accident prevention

Accidents are the commonest cause of death among children aged one to five, and are still far too frequent. It is extremely important that everyone knows and abides by safety rules.

- Discuss safety in the home regularly as children's needs change as they grow up.
- Talk to children about what to do in an emergency such as a fire.
- Try to encourage every member of the family to be tidy and aware of hazards that may cause accidents.
- Teach children to dial 999.
- Help them to know, and to be able to recite, the address of where they are staying.

The pictures on pages 141–142 of living room and kitchen 'dangers' can be used to teach children about different dangers.

You could also get children to draw pictures showing safe rooms and gardens. They could colour in the pictures and also say what is wrong and how things should be.

In the home: general

- Do not buy second hand items unless it is essential. If you do, you must obtain the instruction leaflet or manual and ensure it is correctly installed and used.
- Alcohol, bleach, household chemicals, washing up liquid, and toilet cleaning materials are all poisonous to children. A young girl died recently after drinking a large glass of whisky. Her father had put it by the side of his chair and fallen asleep. Keep everything in a locked cupboard.
- Never expect young children to take responsibility for toddlers or babies inside or outside the home.
- Do not give small children peanuts, chewing gum, or coconut.
- Plastic bags, ribbons and strings should be kept away from young children.
- Young children often put small objects including peanuts into their mouth, nose and ears: be vigilant.
- Don't let young children walk around carrying anything made of glass, or other sharp objects including pencils.
- Teach children not to put anything other than food or drink in their mouths. Watch out for lolly sticks or pencils in mouths.
- Keep matches and lighters out of reach.
- Alcohol should be stored safely away.
- Teach children about the dangers of water and get them to learn to swim as early as possible.
- Don't use juice bottles to store substances other than those for which they were intended.

Example

Sarah came home very thirsty from school, saw a bottle of 'Coke' on the kitchen table and took a quick drink from the bottle. She immediately spat it out. It was wood dye mixture. A quick telephone call to the provider and then to the hospital confirmed that the contents, on this occasion, were not poisonous. The event is a very real reminder of what not to do, but she was lucky!

- Teach children safe cooking habits from an early age.
- Tidying up should be part of every activity for children and adults. In this way stairs will be kept clear, dangerous objects won't be left lying around and unsuitable toys will not be left near young children.
- Take care with DIY, both when doing it and afterwards by ensuring things are safe and tools are carefully collected up and put away.
- Smoke detectors should be checked regularly including batteries.
- Fire extinguishers should be readily available and up-to-date, as should fire blankets.
- A suitable first aid box should also be in the house.

Electrical safety

- Regularly check all electrical appliances for external damage and immediately replace cracked and broken casings, broken plugs and worn flexes.
- There should be no trailing leads anywhere in the house.
- Do not let children turn electrical equipment off or on.
- Do not overload sockets with more appliances than the outlet will cope with.
- Never leave a table or standard lamp plugged in without a light bulb fitted.
- Know which fuse each appliance requires and ensure only the correct fuse is used at all times.
- Never use an iron or ironing board with a small child, toddler or baby around.
- Use socket covers or guards when plug sockets are not in use.

Gas safety

- All appliances should be serviced at least once a year by a CORGI (Council of Registered Gas Installers) service engineer. There may be a serious risk of carbon monoxide poisoning.

> **You cannot see, smell or taste carbon monoxide.**

Fires, heaters, radiators

- Make sure all heaters and fires are fitted with fireguards which are secured to the wall. Do not hang or lean things on fireguards.
- Buy flame retardant night clothes.
- Read the labels on the equipment, know the instructions and keep them for future reference.
- Calor gas fires can tip over. Keep them out of reach of children. They also use up oxygen in the air so they should not be used for long periods.

Furniture

- Is it safely positioned?
- It must only be made of fire resistant foam.
- Glass top tables and coffee tables must be made of safety glass or have film on them.
- Do not allow children to use beds or sofas as trampolines.
- Read the labels on all equipment, know the instructions and keep them handy for future reference.

Stairs

- Fit a safety gate at the top and bottom of the stairs.
- Check banister areas, board up if necessary.
- Make sure floor covering or carpet is secure.
- Do not leave anything on the stairs including toys, shoes or clothes.

Floors

- Wipe up spills at once.
- Do not polish the floor.
- Do not use scatter rugs.
- Check the lino and carpet for damage or cuts.
- Check for any broken floor tiles.

Doors and windows

These should have:
- secure locks and bolts
- door viewer
- door chain
- safety glass or film on glass areas that are at child height

Toys

- Dispose of any broken or dangerous toys.
- Encourage children to help tidy up and put the toys away safely.
- Be aware of the toy safety symbols.
- Encourage older children not to leave small toy pieces around, e.g. lego, pegs.
- Always buy the correct toy for the age of the child.
- Baby walkers can be dangerous: their wheels may jam and the walker will topple over.

Pets

- Never leave babies, toddlers or young children alone with pets, especially cats, dogs and exotic pets.
- Make sure you have time and space for your pet.
- Don't leave pet food around.
- Always use separate dishes, bowls and towels. Wash and clean them separately.
- Don't let pets roam around the kitchen.

In the kitchen

- Get down to the child's height so you can see what they can see and touch. You will notice the dangers then.
- Only have a short or coiled flex on a kettle.
- Always turn pan handles inwards on a cooker.
- Make sure you use cupboard and drawer locks and a fridge lock.
- Never leave children alone in a kitchen.
- Never leave opened tins in a fridge.
- Empty bins regularly.
- Do not let children play in or around waste bins, they make take things out.
- Always fill chip pans $1/3$ full only and never leave pan unattended.
- Always secure child into highchair with harness or reins.

- Keep sharp items such as knives, cutlery, glasses, grater etc. out of reach.
- Store food safely.
- Keep raw and cooked meats separately in the fridge.
- Never walk around with hot drinks when children are around.
- Never have a child on your lap when you are having a hot drink.
- Do not use tablecloths with toddlers or babies around.
- Hob guards around the cooker top are not recommended. They get very hot. Also it makes it more difficult to remove the pan from the cooker over the top of the guard.

In the bathroom and toilet

- Make sure razors and scissors are out of reach.
- Electrical items must be operated by a pull cord only.
- Use only a special shaver socket for electric razors.
- Always run cold water into the bath or sink before running the hot.
- Never leave the child in the bath on their own, even for a few seconds. Collect up all the things you will need before putting the child into the bath.
- Encourage children to wash their hands before they eat and after using the toilet.
- Medicines, pills and tablets must be kept in a locked cabinet.

In the bedrooms

- Always use safe nursery equipment e.g. new mattress in a cot.
- Do not use cot bumper, baby rest, pillows or duvet for babies.
- Do not put the cot or bed next to a radiator or under a window.
- If you have bunk beds, make sure the ladder is secure.
- Do not position furniture near or under a window, the child will be able to climb up.
- Never leave baby on a bed or table on its own.
- Remember do not let the baby sleep with an adult or older children as they may roll onto the baby and crush or suffocate it.

In the garden

- Fencing and gates must be secure, in good repair and designed to prevent children climbing over or opening them.
- Gates should be securely bolted.
- Play equipment such as swings or slides should be secured to the ground over a soft surface and checked regularly.
- Sandpits should be covered when not in use and children supervised whilst playing in them.
- When using electric lawnmowers, hedge trimmers or power tools always use a circuit breaker (RCD). This goes into the wall socket and you then plug the appliance you are using into the RCD.
- Sheds and garages should be kept locked.
- Keep garden tools and chemicals locked away.
- Balconies should be boarded up.
- Ensure garden ponds, water butts etc. are securely covered.
- Barbecues should be supervised by an adult at all times.
- Children should be constantly supervised if using a paddling pool.
- Teach children not to eat or pick berries or plants.

Visiting other people's houses

Extra care should be taken if visiting relatives, friends or other people's property. Check everywhere that there are no visible or hidden dangers.

Example

I took my grandchild to visit a friend who didn't have children. I checked the house and the garden. Unfortunately I didn't look behind the dustbin where there was a paint brush soaking in white spirit. My 18 month old grandson of course found it and we spent a very harrowing day at the local hospital. Had it been something more noxious the outcome could have been disastrous.

In the street

- Use walking reins or hold a toddler's hand.
- Teach children the Green Cross Code.
- Cycle helmets are essential when riding bikes.
- Children should take a cycling proficiency test before being allowed out alone on a bike.
- Make regular safety checks on the bike.
- Be sure the child can be seen when walking or riding, use fluorescent clothing or armbands.

In the car

Special baby seats, car seats, seat belts, booster seats, carry cot belts must be used. Check regularly for wear or fault. Follow the makers instructions about the age and weight of children using the seat.

Sleep

No two children need exactly the same amount of sleep but regular sleep is essential. You cannot make a child go to sleep at night but they are more likely to sleep if they have:

- plenty of exercise and fresh air
- plenty to eat
- plenty of play and things to do in the day

Make going to bed a happy time, and it helps to have a bedtime routine. Here are some ideas:

- a quiet time before bed
- a warm bath
- a warm milky drink
- a goodnight story, song, talk and cuddle
- a favourite toy
- things to look at in bed until sleepy

If the child wakes in the night reassure them firmly and quietly, but it is best not to talk or play or to give them drinks because they will enjoy this and will be more likely to go on waking up. If the child always wakes early leave sturdy picture books and safe toys for them to play with. If the child is awake a lot and you feel tired or worried, talk it over with your health visitor or school nurse.

Research has shown that children who have been under stress or who have experienced loss or separation may not sleep well (*Through the Night* by Dilys Daws). It may just be that the child is used to very different sleeping arrangements to what others consider 'normal'.

Patience, understanding, talking and listening are the best tools. Gradually the child should develop better sleeping habits. Children can suffer from nightmares or they can experience night terrors: either can occur without being caused by any emotional upset. A **nightmare** results in the child being awake and aware. A **night terror** is when the child appears to be terrified but is unaware of your presence.

If however, things don't improve or the child continues to have nightmares, you may need to seek professional help.

Cot death is most likely to occur in children under six months. The key precautions to take are:

- Avoid smoking at any time near the baby or in the room where the baby will go.
- Back to sleep (lay the baby on his back when putting him down to sleep).
- Feet to foot (put the child's feet at the foot of the bed).
- Room temperature should be kept constant at around 18°C.
- Do not over wrap the child: overwrapping the child can cause the child to overheat.
- Do not use cot bumpers or quilts.

Smoking

It is important for everyone to know, and to remember, that:
1. Smoking is one of the greatest hazards to human health today.
2. The majority of smokers begin in childhood.

Children should have the right to:
- be free from the effects of tobacco when in their mother's womb
- be brought up in a home that is smoke free
- expect that doctors, teachers and all those caring for them will set a good example by not smoking
- schools, youth clubs and public places that are smoke free
- be taught about the impact of smoking on health and well-being
- be taught how to recognise and resist pressures to smoke
- not be sold cigarettes and other tobacco products
- be helped to remain non-smokers by the high cost of cigarettes
- be free from any form of tobacco advertising and promotion
- live in a community where non-smoking is the normal way of life for all age groups

What is passive smoking?

Passive smoking is breathing other people's cigarette smoke. Until recently most people were unaware of the dangers. Not only will it cause irritation to eyes, nose and throat, headaches, dizziness and sickness, it can cause asthma and allergies to worsen and increase the risk of cancer by up to 30 per cent.

> **Roy Castle, the entertainer and presenter of 'Record Breakers' died from lung cancer. He had never smoked. He had worked in a lot of places where other people smoked.**

Speech and language

In many ways, what a person achieves in life depends on how well they communicate. In other words learning to communicate is of great importance to everyone. Too often problems occur because people can't talk to each other. Our whole education system is based on language, both spoken and written. It is therefore never too early to start to help a child develop language skills.

Language and talking should be fun, natural and should take place all the time.

Don't try to change what children have learned already: they'll learn by example. If a carer is worried that a child's speech is not as it should be they can contact the local education authority or health visitor who can offer specialists to help.

At the age of five a child's speech may not be perfect, particularly 'r' and 'th'—indeed, these sounds may never be formed properly.

What is important is that a child's language and vocabulary has had a chance to develop outside the home by:
- looking at and reading books
- talking about events and everyday activities
- experiences such as visits, cooking, playgroups, toddlers groups, school, clubs
- mixing as much as possible with other children

As a rough guide:
- At 18 months a child should have a few words.
- By two years, they should know around 50 words and be beginning to put two words together.
- By three years, they should be quite chatty, starting conversations, asking questions, their speech becoming clear with continued increase in language skills throughout the early years.

Many people misinterpret a speech or language problem as laziness or being naughty.
- Does the child have difficulty following instructions without visible clues such as pointing?
- Does the child not hear if spoken to from behind?
- Does the child have a problem understanding what is being said?
- Does the child have difficulty expressing ideas in words and rely on non-verbal communication such as pointing or taking you to things?
- Does the child rely on a brother or sister to translate for them or not bother to try to understand?
- Is the child's speech difficult to understand in comparison to children of the same age?

If you think there is a problem, ask for help sooner rather than later.

One in twenty children will experience what appears to be stuttering or stammering. To help them come through this without developing a permanent stammer, don't react or tell them to slow down. Ignore it. These periods of stammering sometimes start as a result of major life changes such as starting school or going 'into care'. Most will stop within three months but if not seek advice.

How can carers help children develop speech and language skills?

- Talk to them as much as possible.
- Include them in conversations.
- Ask questions.
- Be patient; wait for their answers.
- Listen to the child and respond.
- Say the correct sentence or word.
- Don't put them under pressure or demand speech.

If a child has difficulty with:

Speech: If a child says 'tar' for 'car', don't say that's wrong, but repeat the word correctly. 'Tan I pay tars, pease?'

Response: 'Yes, you can play cars. Get the cars out, please.'

Expression: If a child asks for a toy by pointing to it and saying 'Get it' because he does not know the word.

Response: 'What do you want? The tiger? Let's get the tiger. There he is, tiger.'

Understanding: If a child, when asked to put the box under the table, puts the box on the table

Response: 'Put it under the table (pointing). Well done. The box is under the table.'

The more talking and repeating correctly children hear the more confident they will become and their speech and language will develop naturally.

Watching TV alone or with other children will not often help develop children's language skills. They may be entertained but they will not develop language skills unless an adult sits with them and talks about what they have seen afterwards.

Accents and dialects

Accents and dialects are very valuable parts of everyone's heritage and must be respected, preserved and valued. Children must learn to communicate in the same way as the community in which they belong. This may sometimes be difficult for carers to accept, wanting to correct a grammatically incorrect sentence such as:

'I ain't got no money.'

All children should learn standard English and be able to use different language styles depending on the situation, as we all do everyday.

As children get older they often pick up words, phrases and language that may fill their parents and carers with horror. This is a natural part of their development and if ignored will usually soon disappear.

Suntan

It has now been proved that spending too much time in the sun is not a good idea and can cause skin cancer.

Babies under one year (and preferably all children under two years) should not be exposed to the sun at all. They should be shaded with a hat, a parasol and clothes. Sun block should also be worn.

Over exposure to the sun is not good for anyone and can increase the risk of malignant melanoma (skin cancer) even if a sun cream is used. However, the following tips should be used as a guide if a child is going to be out in the sun.
- Tan slowly, gradually increasing the time spent in the sun each day.
- Always use the appropriate sunscreens for different types of skin (e.g. Factor 15 or 25 and so on) but never on babies under three months.
- Avoid the midday sun.
- Wear a sun hat.
- Wear a good pair of sunglasses.
- Above all don't burn, tan slowly.

Everyone's skin can burn but people with fair skin, usually those with blond or red hair, are particularly vulnerable. African, Caribbean and Asian skins also burn and need protection as most black children who are fostered are born in this country.

In Australia they have developed the following code which might help:

Slip	'T' shirt on
Slop	suncream on
Slap	hat on

Temper tantrums

Temper tantrums usually occur between one and three years of age. As children get minds of their own and learn to say 'No' they may scream and throw themselves about in temper. Temper tantrums are also very common amongst children who are looked after, especially if they are emotionally disturbed or feel very insecure. It happens most when:

- you and the child are tired
- the child is hungry
- the child cannot do what they want
- the child is not getting much attention
- the child is being hurried

You will get to know what starts the child off. If you can see a tantrum starting, try to take the child's mind off it by providing something else to do.

If the child has a tantrum:

- Check that they are in a safe place.
- Try to stay calm and not take too much notice.
- Don't smack, it will only make it worse.
- Don't give in!

Afterwards, when the time is right, the carer may want to try to talk to the child about what is acceptable.

Toilet training

Wetting: daytime

Most children are more or less dry by day by the age of three, whether they've been trained or not. But lots of children go on wetting at night for some time after this. Lots of parents or carers search for some way of training children to be dry as early as possible, really because it means less work. Most parents or carers with other children would say that the only thing you can do about wetting, either by day or by night, is put up with it.

If a child starts wetting after having become reliably dry or has never been dry in the day by the age of 4–5 years, advice should be sought as this could be due to an infection or other treatable cause. It may also be due to an emotional problem. Many local authority areas now offer an enuretic service for children over eight years with wetting problems. This is usually run by school nurses.

Bedwetting

Some children are dry at night by three years but many will take longer. A child cannot help bedwetting. They are not being lazy. One in six of all five-year-olds still wets the bed, especially boys. If carers are worried, they should talk to their doctor or health visitor. The following may be helpful:

- Reduce the size of the child's drink towards the end of the day.
- Don't give drinks in bed.
- Get them to use the toilet before they get undressed.
- Just before they get into bed, get them to try to go again.
- When you go to bed, carefully lift and take the child to the toilet again.
- If they wake and want a drink, give them just a very small drink of water.
- Above all, don't get angry or show your anxiety.

If bedwetting happens after the child has become reliably dry at night, it is important to make sure that there is not a urine infection present, which needs treating, before putting it down to emotional upset.

When a child is about eight years old and still wetting the bed some authorities may provide a night alarm to wake the child.

Constipation, soiling and smearing

Make sure the child isn't frightened. Reassure. Let the child be with you when you go to the toilet. Try to be as relaxed as you can be about the problem.

Make sure the child eats plenty of fibre from wholemeal bread, chapattis, wholegrain breakfast cereals, fruit and vegetables. Baked beans, frozen peas and sweetcorn are good sources of fibre often liked by children. Also give lots to drink, clear drinks rather than milk. All this will help to prevent constipation.

Soiling is often associated with constipation. If a child becomes frightened of the toilet they can 'hang on' to their stools. This makes them constipated. A doctor can help by giving a child a mild laxative.

Constipation, soiling pants or smearing of excreta sometimes happens when a child is upset about something. All you may be able to do is help the child feel as happy and secure as possible day to day, and wait for the problem to pass. But if it continues and you're worried, talk to your health visitor, doctor or social worker

Weaning

The present Department of Health Guidelines recommend that weaning should be discouraged before four months and not delayed beyond six months of age.

Things for children to do to help them learn about safety. Talking is also a good idea too.

Colour the pictures and then:

Activity 13: Spot the living room dangers

Child playing with plug and socket.

Mug of hot coffee balanced on chair arm.

Vacuum cleaner flex frayed and left trailing on floor.

Scissors left on table.

Insecticide spray on low table.

Lighted cigarette fallen into upholstered chair.

Hot iron left face down on ironing board.

Flex of iron draped low in reach of a child.

Standard lamp's flex trailing across room.

Child playing with matches.

Hearth rug rucked up.

Clothes drying too close to fire.

No guard surround in front of fire.

Mirror above fire place.

Meths and paper left too close to fire.

Activity 14: Spot the kitchen dangers

Child left alone in kitchen.
Child left to touch oven door.
Chip pan left unattended.
Chip pan handle sticking out over edge of cooker.
Cat left to roam around kitchen.
Kettle flex overhanging edge of worktop.
Overloading of plug socket with appliances.
Washing machine door left open.
Bowl of liquid left on floor.
Spilt liquid left on floor and not mopped up.
Cupboard doors left open.
Disinfectant bottle in easy reach of child.
Sharp knife left near edge of worktop.
Open bottles of pills in low cupboard.
Open bin revealing sharp objects.
Broken glass on floor.

Together, children and carers could carry out a check for dangers around the house.

The following two lists show other dangers. A child could draw a picture of a garden and also one of the countryside. When the child has finished the carer and child could check together that none of the dangers mentioned below is included.

Activity 15: Spot the garden dangers

Untidy garden shed (falling objects).

Nails sticking out of piece of wood.

Chemical left in reach of children.

Garden rake left on ground.

Uneven, cracked paving slabs.

Toys left on garden path.

Very small child left unattended in paddling pool.

Paraffin should not be used to light fires; it has also been left too close to the bonfire.

Bonfire left unattended and also too close to shed and fence.

Child playing with deck chair.

Man overreaching with electric hedge trimmer.

Dustbin lid has been left off revealing sharp objects.

Back gate left open.

Ladder at too steep an angle.

Man too far up ladder and overreaching.

Child playing too close to patio doors.

Girl using sharp knife to clean lawn mower while it is still plugged in.

Activity 16: Spot the countryside dangers

Poking wasps nest with sticks.

Child climbing tree overhanging rocks near lake.

Children playing too close to railway.

Flying kites near overhead cables

Litter left lying on ground.

Child running bare foot.

Child left unattended in lake (drowning).

Child messing about on water.

Child in boat not wearing a life belt.

Child eating berries (poisoning).

Activity 17: Bathroom poisons wordsearch

```
c m a a m b u l a n c e c d p
a a e w b e l t t f b a o i a
b s o d o c t o r l o f n s r
i p c h i l d p g o t t t i a
n i s v s c j r q j t e a n c
e r a t n s i u m r l r i f e
t i f q e r x n s c e s n e t
l n e m l o c k e z t h e c a
z v u w b z a x y e y a r t m
t f c c d b l d a a k v z a o
i l s y r u p h g n f e e n l
r c d i u e o f j e g k y t h
s i n k g j l h o s p i t a l
o p o i s o n i w i d s a l p
h p i l l s b l e a c h x v r
```

Can you find the words below in the box?

aftershave	child	medicine
ambulance	disinfectant	paracetamol
aspirin	doctor	pills
bottle	drugs	poison
bleach	fumes	safe
cabinet	hospital	sink
calpol	key	syrup
container	lock	

Activity 18: Garden poisons wordsearch

s	l	u	g	p	e	l	l	e	t	s	p
p	a	r	a	f	f	i	n	b	l	i	o
u	e	w	c	l	p	v	b	e	u	a	i
w	h	i	t	e	s	p	i	r	i	t	s
t	x	e	t	a	d	s	p	r	u	t	o
f	s	r	f	d	g	p	a	i	n	t	n
h	o	s	p	i	t	a	l	e	h	r	h
l	i	q	y	c	i	b	i	s	a	f	e
b	o	t	t	l	e	j	d	g	a	p	j
w	o	o	d	f	i	l	l	e	r	k	o
a	n	t	k	i	l	l	e	r	l	z	o
w	e	e	d	k	i	l	l	e	r	m	k

Can you find the words below in the box?

ant killer	oil	slugpellets
berries	paint	turps
bottle	paraffin	weed killer
hospital	petrol	white spirit
lead	poison	wood filler

Activity 19: Kitchen poisons wordsearch

```
w a x t z p q s c f m l b y w x l c n
i a l c o h o l j u a o p v r o m o p
n d s c a z b l s m p x q t y r n n a
e b f h n h i i l e r b p a q r s t z
v l i o i l m p a s c e o g i k m a o
p e r s a n b n g i c e f a c o h i d
e a s p l a g e r f p i b j r g q n h
i c t i j r j u k s k i d a k d f e l
m h a t n t l l p o v m o z m d p r q
r v i a s w n n a l t l o c k i u x o
v y d l c b e e r w i x z o e s y a p
q p k z a o a b a b c q c d y i d e r
s f i e t t f t c g g u u h h n i v q
x j t j c t k w e l p m c i n f o l d
c p m y h l q n t r o o h s d f t p o
a u w a u e v t e w z s i x r c y q c
l z w b r x f y m a x f l s b t s c t
p d t i w s d a o e c z d f o a g y o
o h b e t g j v l i c f u h f n j d r
l a m b u l a n c e k g f e l t m e h
```

Can you find the words below in the box?

alcohol	catch	first aid kit	pills
ambulance	child	fumes	poison
beer	container	hospital	safe
bleach	cupboard	key	washing up liquid
bottle	disinfectant	lock	wine
calpol	doctor	paracetamol	

Activity 20: Health quiz

Together carers and children could find the answers to these questions in the chapter on health.

1. Give three reasons why being healthy is important?

2. What are Milestones?

3. Walkmans damage ears. How long does it take for ears to become damaged?

4. What else can damage your ears?

5. Why should:

    - teeth be checked and cleaned regularly?
    - eyes be checked?
    - weight be checked?
    - feet be measured?
    - height be measured?

6. a) List five healthy foods

   b) five unhealthy foods

7. Why are the following harmful?
    smoking
    drinking alcohol
    drug taking
    solvent abuse

8. Which four things do you think are most important as far as children's rights and smoking are concerned?

9. Draw a picture which shows the Australian slogan on sunbathing

10. Name at least two things that should be on a health record sheet

Activity 21: Milestones

Child's name:

First:	age:	date:
Smiled		
Made cooing noises		
Rolled over		
Sat up alone		
Crawled		
Pulled up on the furniture		
Walked alone		
Ate with a hand		
Ate with spoon		
Said first proper word (not mama, dada) in first language		
Put two or three words together in first language		
Was dry during the day		
Was clean (toilet trained)		
Was dry at night		
Kicked a ball		
Pedalled a tricycle		
Could name three colours in first language		
Are there any other events you want to record?		
Perhaps finding out is something you and the child could do together?		

Name of Health visitor: ....

Telephone no: ....

Activity 22: Health record sheet

Child's name: ....

Name and address of doctor: ....

Telephone number: ....

Visits to the family doctor:

Treatment	Date

Record of injections (immunisation)

Type of injection	Date

Childhood illnesses such as tummy upsets, ear ache etc. when doctor has not seen the child.

Illness	Date

Clinic visits for particular reasons such as developmental checks, hearing, vision, speech therapy

Clinic visits	Date

Hospital visits and stays

Hospital visits	Illness/Operation	Date

Name and address of **dentist**: ....

Telephone number: ....

Visits to the dentist

Treatment	Date

Name and address of **optician**: ....

Telephone number: ....

Visits to the optician

Treatment/Advice	Date

Section 8: Meetings

Meetings, meetings, meetings. There are so many different meetings which often seem to be a waste of time.

Meetings are useful for:
- obtaining information
- sharing views
- solving problems
- reaching decisions
- making plans
- checking progress
- gaining consensus

To be effective meetings need to achieve their aim in a reasonable way in a reasonable time leaving a trail of clear crisp decisions.

Preparing for meetings

Successful meetings depend upon good detailed planning; who needs to attend and what preparation do they need before taking part. This matters as much as the conduct of the meeting itself.

It is a good idea to go over details of the meeting with the child beforehand and to prepare them as much as possible. Talk about what questions they may want to ask and the best way to do so. Find out if the child would like someone to speak on their behalf at the meeting. The child could alternatively tape record what they want to say or write a letter.

Let the child know that their contribution will be welcome and valued. Children are much more likely to take part in the meeting if they can see the purpose and feel it will be worthwhile.

The following may be useful for whoever is organising the meeting. It will also help carers to know what to expect. If you do not think a meeting is being organised well, you should contact the chair to discuss your concerns.

The meeting should include an interpreter to support the family or the child if this is appropriate. Social services can give guidance.

Whether smoking is allowed in a meeting should be decided beforehand and the decision stated at least before the meeting begins. If it is decided that smoking will not be allowed then the chair should remind everyone at the beginning of the meeting. For some people a no smoking rule will be difficult and it may be possible for the chair to organise brief breaks where smokers can go outside to smoke.

Time and date

- All meetings should be arranged so that the child can easily attend and misses as little schooling as possible.
- Always try to set the date for the next meeting before closing the present meeting if you can.

Place

Sometimes parents, carers or children do not feel comfortable on social services department premises. Important meetings can take place anywhere, such as carers' or parents' home.

Choose a venue that is suitable for the occasion and prepare the room well before the meeting begins so that if anyone arrives early they have somewhere to go.

- How should the chairs and, if needed, any tables be laid out?
- Would comfortable chairs and coffee tables be better?
- What equipment is needed e.g. tape recorder, flip chart?
- Does the meeting need to be on neutral ground?
- Is the environment pleasant and suitable for the occasion?
- Is access easy? Is there disabled access?
- Is there parking available or is there public transport close by?
- Will anyone require transport or child care, or their expenses paid in advance?
- Will anyone need an interpreter?

Agenda

- This should be prepared and if possible circulated beforehand. It should identify the topics to be considered and also who is to introduce the topic, such as a specialist on a particular topic. It is more important to examine the future than to go back over the past. Though a review must look at recent care, it is important not to dwell on the past but to look forward positively.
- Don't have too many items. A long agenda is tiring and boring and items will not get the attention they deserve.
- If the meeting is informal, let those present know what you want to discuss before you begin. One idea is to agree the agenda for the next meeting at the end of the present meeting.

Time-keeping

- A prompt start makes good use of the time available. Any delay in starting encourages people to arrive late in the future.
- Breaks are useful to divide up different topics and prevent boredom. If you are chairing the meeting do control the length of breaks and keep pressure up on progress.
- Start by making it clear when the meeting will end and keep to that time. We owe it to other people to make the best use of their time.
- Announce approximately ten minutes before the end that the meeting is drawing to a close.

Minutes or notes

Unfortunately minutes are often used as a form of 'protection or insurance'. They therefore contain a lot about 'who said what'. The importance of minutes is that they record decisions reached and actions planned. In other words **who is to do what and by when**.

Reviewing minutes of meetings is then confined to checking whether people have done what they promised.

Size of meetings

A meeting needs to be manageable. Large meetings may prevent full contributions and become more formal. Small meetings may have limited expertise, but are less formal. Only people directly concerned should attend, providing they have the necessary authority to make decisions.

One way of keeping attendance to a reasonable number is to have people attend solely for the items which concern them. Remember: a lot of people in one place may be daunting or distressing for a child.

The meeting

Make sure the child sits in a suitable place and if the child wishes, you should sit next to them. It may be that the parents will want the child to sit next to them. Have ready:

- Ideas you think will help the child.
- Strategies to help the child say what they think.
- Thoughts on what should be done if someone attends the meeting whom the child doesn't wish to see e.g. step-mother, teacher.
- Ways to ensure everyone present has the opportunity to speak or record their thoughts, comments or feelings.
- Ideas on how to handle and record disagreements if the child, family or carer don't agree with what is being said.
- Strategies to ensure the meeting is not discriminatory e.g. *'kids in care always do badly at school'*. This could be turned into a positive point by asking the social worker to explain what steps are being taken to help the child catch up with their school work.

Would providing refreshments help the meeting or would it be a distraction? Plan accordingly.

End of the meeting

- Check to see that the child, and the parents and carers have said what they want to say and that everyone understands the confidentiality of what has been discussed.
- Make sure the meeting ends with a positive feeling and with clearly agreed aims and objectives.
- Summarise what has taken place.
- Who will do what and by when including passing on information to those not present.
- Set the date for the next meeting.
- Finish on time.

Planning meetings

Every child who is looked after by the local authority should have an up-to date plan so that they know where they stand and what it is hoped will happen to them in the future.

Providing the child is old enough to understand, they should take part in making this plan which will then have their commitment. In some cases an interpreter may be needed. Your local authority will give guidance on this.

Sometimes the first planning meeting takes place before the child leaves home but if not as soon as possible afterwards. If the child does not have a plan, the carer should press for one to be prepared as soon as possible.

What will be on the plan?

- What the child's needs are including health, diet, religion, language, education, friends, carers. This may mean finding out where particular shops sell, for example, Afro-Caribbean food or where a synagogue or mosque is located.
- If a child is disabled what extra help they need.
- Where the child will be living.
- If it is possible to predict how long the child is likely to be looked after by social services.
- What should happen in the future, and when it will happen.
- When the child will see their parents and how the parents will be involved.
- What will happen if things don't work out as planned.
- Arrangements for education and health care.
- Who is responsible for carrying out the different parts of the plan.

There is a standard form for this information.

Who goes to a planning meeting?

Whenever possible:
- the child
- the parents
- the social worker
- anyone else who cares about the child such as grandparents, aunts, uncles, friends
- anyone who works with the child
- foster carer or key worker
- other people may be invited such as teachers, doctors, educational welfare officers, interpreters

Can a child speak at the meeting?

Encourage the child to say what they think and to be part of any decisions made. The child should be prepared before the meeting so they can take an active part in discussions.

Children may ask for some members of the group to leave the room for a time if they feel uncomfortable speaking in front of them. Others can also ask for the child to leave the room when it is their turn to speak.

What happens next?

The agreed plan and any decisions made in the meeting will be written down and everybody who was invited should be given a copy, including the child.

Further planning meetings may be called later to see how things are progressing.

As it is not always easy to put the plan into action quickly, carers will need to tell the child what is going on as well as to encourage the child to talk about any worries.

Reviews

Reviews are very important for children even though quite often they don't realise it. A child should be encouraged to attend whenever possible and if they can't attend, to send their apologies and to find another way of passing on their views or comments.

Reviews are where important decisions about a child's plans take place.

Whoever is responsible for organising a child's review should make sure that the time and place is suitable for everyone especially the child. It is, after all, their review. A child can, if they wish, ask for a review to take place.

What are reviews?

Reviews are regular meetings which social services must hold for all children who are looked after by them.

A review is held:
- To ensure a child is being cared for properly.
- To make sure that the plans made for the child are being carried out.
- To decide whether the plans should be changed in any way.

How often do they happen?

A review must be held within four weeks of when a child is first looked after; then within three months; then within six months. If a lot is happening or there is a problem then reviews may be held more often.

Must a child go to them?

It's a very good idea for the child to attend if they are old enough to understand as they can have their say about what's going on. Encourage the child to speak up, or make suggestions or get someone else to speak for them. This can be a friend or someone they can trust. A child should be helped before the meeting with explanations of what and why things will be discussed.

If it really isn't possible for the child to attend their review or the child doesn't wish to attend they can write down what they want to say and ask someone else to read it for them or they could make a tape or write a letter.

Who will be there?

All the people who are concerned about the child should be there including their parents, carer, social worker and sometimes teacher and interpreter if appropriate.

If at the review, the child doesn't want to say what they feel in front of their parents, they can ask for them to leave the room. The parents might also ask for the child to leave the room whilst they have their say. If it is known that this might happen it is a good idea to tell either the child or the parents in advance.

What happens before the review?

The child will be asked:
- how they are getting on
- what they want to happen
- anything else they would like to talk about at the review

A child can write this down or get someone else to write it for them. Their social worker and carer will also be asked to write down what they think as well. Everyone should see what the others have written before the review.

Will someone take notes of what is said at the meeting?

Yes, and everyone including the child should get a copy. If a child is not happy with the notes they should tell their carer or their social worker.

The carer should help the child to follow up matters, if what has been agreed doesn't happen within a reasonable amount of time. The time for something to happen or action to be taken should be agreed at the review.

Disruption meetings: when a placement breaks down

When a placement breaks down a disruption meeting should be called to:
- Help the child or young person by understanding their needs better.
- Improve practice by understanding what went wrong.
- Recognise all the positive work and good experiences for the child amongst the difficulties.
- Support everyone and help them to carry on and recover.
- Demonstrate that disruption is never the fault of one or two people, or the result of a single factor.

A placement breakdown is invariably the outcome of a whole series of connected factors.

Who should be present?

There should always be an independent chairperson, who has not been connected with the placement.

Those who should attend include:
- the adoptive parents or foster carers
- the present carers unless this is too difficult for the previous carers
- all social workers who have been involved in the placement
- those social workers currently responsible for the child or young person
- the team manager
- someone to take minutes of the meeting

It may be appropriate to include a therapist, but not teachers or other professionals. A child or young person rarely attends. Members of the birth family do not attend unless they are the carers.

Agenda for disruption meetings

The following should be considered in sequence:
1. The child or young person's early history before being looked after by the local authority.
2. Care history, before this placement.
3. The assessment and preparation of the child or young person and the panel decision to place.
4. The assessment and preparation of the applicants, and the panel decision.
5. The matching of the child and family, and the panel decision.
6. The introductory period.
7. The actual placement.
8. What has happened since the placement disrupted.
9. The child's current priority needs.

Note: *disruption meetings are not planning meetings for the future.*

Report of the disruption meeting

The report should be distributed to everyone who was invited to the meeting. It should only be given to specified other people with the agreement of those at the meeting.

Organisation of disruption meetings

The child's social worker is usually responsible for organising the meeting. Each meeting usually lasts approximately five hours.

Family group conferences

Family group conferences are meetings set up to assist a family in drawing up a plan for the care of a child. A typical model might be:

a) Referral
Agree the need for a plan. A co-ordinator is appointed who is matched with the family's race, culture, language and religion.

b) Stage One
The co-ordinator, in consultation with the child and their immediate carers, identifies the 'family', issues invitations, agrees venues, dates and timing, and prepares the participants.

c) Stage Two
At the start of the meeting the co-ordinator chairs the information-sharing. Professionals explain their roles, responsibilities and concerns and local resources. The family can seek clarification.

d) Stage Three

This is a private planning time for the family when the professionals and co-ordinator withdraw. The family needs to agree a plan, contingency plans and to review arrangements.

e) Stage Four

The co-ordinator and the professionals rejoin the family and hear the plan. Resources are negotiated and the plan agreed unless it places the child at risk of significant harm.

Child protection conference

What is a child protection conference?

This is a meeting called if the social services, the police, a teacher or someone from the health service such as a doctor thinks a child may be suffering, or at serious risk of suffering, significant harm because of physical injury or neglect or sexual abuse or emotional abuse, and may need protection.

Who goes to a child protection conference?

Any of the following may attend:
- the child (if they are old enough to understand)
- their parents
- if the child is being looked after, their carer
- their social worker and other social service officers
- the police
- a teacher
- a doctor or specialist
- the health visitor
- lawyers on all sides

A friend or someone the child trusts may be there or may speak on their behalf and the child should be told about the meeting.

A member of staff from the social services department usually chairs the meeting and a specially trained clerk will be in attendance to take the minutes.

Who gets a copy of the minutes?

Everyone present at the meeting will get a copy. The reasons for any decisions made must be clearly stated. If the parents are only present for part of the time they will often only be given the minutes for that part of the meeting.

What happens at the meeting?

The first child protection conference is called to exchange information and to decide whether the child should be placed on the Child Protection Register.

If so, then a keyworker will be appointed to:
- co-ordinate a plan
- help the child and parents to take part in the plan
- keep the child informed of what is going on

The plan is made to ensure the child is kept safe and well and that they get any help needed. The plan will also show any other action that may be necessary. Whatever is agreed at the meeting should be carefully explained to the child.

What is the Child Protection Register?

It is a list of children and young people who are considered to be suffering or who are likely to suffer significant harm. The reason for a child's name appearing on the register should be explained to the child.

Why is there a list?

To provide:
- A register of all children and young people in the area whom it is thought may be at risk, or who are at risk.
- A central point of reference for professional staff who are worried about a child and want to know quickly whether a child protection plan exists.
- Information for all the professionals concerned.

When can the child's name come off the list?

- If the plan made at the child protection conference is successful and it is thought that a child is no longer at risk.
- If the reasons which originally led to the registration no longer apply.
- If the child has moved to another area and that area has accepted responsibility for the case.
- When the young person is 18 years old.
- If the young person has got married.
- When the child has died.

The first two categories for de-registration always require a conference to take place. All other categories may be agreed without a meeting.

How often do these meetings take place?

They must be held at least every six months to review the situation and more often if necessary until such time as everyone agrees they are no longer required.

For further information, see the child protection procedures. All professionals should be familiar with these procedures and have easy access to them. Different local authorities involve key workers and carers differently in child protection and post-child protection work.

Who's who in helping children

The best helpers are often the child's family and friends. But the following may also be involved; however, they may be known by other names in different regions.

Foster carer (may be known as family based carer): Foster carers have an agreement with social services. A child lives in the foster carer's own home. There are many different types of foster carers, all of whom should be trained. Foster carers like to get to know a child really well and help in many different ways.

Key worker: In residential settings the keyworkers are responsible for the children. They build a relationship with the child, assess the child's needs, and help to meet those needs. They are involved with admissions; planning; liaising with other agencies and with parents; for the overall well being of the child.

Field social workers: All children who are being looked after should have a field social worker who is based in the office of the area from which the child came. In some areas they are called care managers. Generally their job is to keep in touch with the child, their family and residential or foster carers and any other interested people, and to make sure plans are carried out.

They usually organise planning meetings and reviews, and handle any court matters for social services departments. The field social worker is the first person the child, residential carer and foster carer should contact for information or final decision making.

Key worker's line manager, supervisor, team manager or head of home: This is the person who is responsible for the key worker. Key workers will go to their line manager for advice and guidance. This person may be the manager of the home. If a child has any difficulties with their key worker, the child should discuss this with another worker or the line manager. The child may need help to do this.

Family placement worker or foster carer's social worker: Most foster carers will have a social worker or link worker who is based in the fostering family placement team. This person advises the foster carer about general fostering issues and organises training.

Team managers, area managers and directors of social services: Most social service departments are organised like pyramids, with team managers, area managers, deputy directors and finally the director. Each level is responsible for the level below. It is a good idea to find out how social services are organised as occasionally you might need the help of someone senior. If there are difficulties with a social worker, carers should contact any of these people.

Children's rights officer (CRO): Some areas have a children's rights officer who is usually independent from social workers. Children in residential and foster care should be able to telephone the CRO and discuss privately anything that is bothering them. If they have a problem, children should also be able to contact Childline or similar organisations listed at the back of this book.

Independent visitor: Children who are not in touch with their families may have an independent visitor.

Family centre or family resource centre workers: Many areas have a family centre where parents are helped and supported in caring for a child.

Complaints officer: Each local authority should have a person appointed to handle complaints from children, families and carers. If a disagreement cannot be sorted out informally with the social worker, team manager or residential staff, carers should contact the complaints officer and ask for the local authority's leaflet on how to make a complaint.

Education welfare officers and educational social workers: Their job is to be a link between the school and the residential or foster home. They talk to the school about any problem a child may be having at school, for example, bullying. They are also involved when a child is truanting. They can usually be contacted through the school.

Educational psychologist: If a child is having real difficulties in learning or concentrating at school, the head teacher may ask for an educational psychologist to see them. An educational psychologist is not a psychiatrist, but someone who has special knowledge about how children learn and what may be causing them to have difficulties. Educational psychologists are involved when children need specific educational help to overcome difficulties.

Child guidance workers and child and family therapy workers: Child guidance workers help children who may have an emotional or behavioural problem perhaps because of some earlier unhappy experience.

A child psychiatrist will be part of the team which includes psychologists and specialist social workers. With the help of the child, their carer or their family, the child guidance worker draws up a plan to overcome the difficulties.

Health visitor: This person is attached to the local GPs surgery or health centre. They work with children under five years old and with families who may need extra help with children over five years. Health visitors are qualified nurses and some are qualified midwives. Carers and parents can contact them at any time at the surgery or health centre. They will make visits to the home if required.

Records

What records do social services keep on a child?

They may keep four sets of records on every child:
1. A straightforward list of who is accommodated or looked after.
2. Case records.
3. Management records.
4. Looking After Children: Assessment and Action Records (LAC). The forms have been produced on behalf of the Department of Health and record a child's progress and what action is necessary and by whom in the future. In addition there are other records available including plan and review records.

What's on these records?

1. **The list shows**:
   - The real name of the child as well as the name they wish to be known by.
   - Where they are staying.
   - Their telephone number.
   - Their date of birth.
   - The name of their social worker.

In most authorities this will be kept on a computer and up-dated either by the social worker or by an administrative assistant.

2. **Case records** should show:
   - All the information in 1. above.
   - Details of the child's family.
   - The child's plan.
   - Any reports written about the child such as court reports, health, home study, etc.
   - Review documents.
   - Details of court orders.
   - Details of arrangements made for contact with the family.
   - Any special arrangements.
   - Any documents used to find out more about the child such as psychological reports or court reports.

The child may also ask to have other documents such as certificates or school reports to be kept with this information.

Children's homes keep records about the child and these are usually very similar to the case records. Foster carers are sometimes given only brief written documents about a child. This depends on the practice of the local authority. However, it is important for the carer to keep their own records for future reference. This could be in the form of a foster carer's diary, listing events, illnesses, accidents as well as specific details about the child.

If the foster carer is involved with the child's court case or accompanies the child to court they may be given a copy of the court order.

3. **Management records** will be the same as case records except that details of the carers will be included.

4. **Looking After Children: Assessment and Action Records (LACs)** are a set of questions covering health, education, identity, family and social relationships, social presentation, emotional and behavioural development and self-care skills. Children should help complete these forms.

These records are used to make sure every step possible is being taken to ensure that the child is developing to the best of their ability. Carers must discuss with the child many topics and *The Foster Carer's Handbook* may be helpful here.

At the end of each section of these records there is a summary of what action needs to be taken, when and by whom.

Can a child see all their records?

Every child has a right to see their records if they wish. There must be a very good reason for anyone saying 'No'. Some records are written by other agencies and may not be made available to the child.

When a child sees their records for the first time, what is written may come as quite a shock and help may be needed to cope with this.

What does a child have to do to see them?

A child should ask their social worker. However, in the past children have not been allowed to see their records so it has come as quite a shock for some social workers and carers to have to change. Some local authorities have introduced systems to make sure only certain people see the records. This, unfortunately, has also made it difficult for the children to see them.

Who else can see them?

All these records are confidential with only authorised staff able to see them. The Case Records and the Management Records should be held in a safe place so that only those people shown below may see them:
- the child
- the child's social worker and superiors
- government inspectors
- the child's guardian ad litem

How long will the records be kept?

The computer records are kept until the child is 23, or if they die before that, for five years after death.

Case records must be kept for 75 years from the date they were started; or for 15 years after the child's death if they die before they are 18 years old.

Activity 23: Who will be at the meeting?

What are the names of the people who will be at the meeting?

....

....

What are their titles, for example, parent, social worker?

....

....

Put the names where you think they will all sit.

You may have to draw some more chairs or a different table.

After the meeting check to see if you were right.

Child's name: ....

Meeting's name: ....

Place: ....

Date: ....

Introduction

Most young people will never attend court in their life. Most will never have a court order that refers to them. Unfortunately this is not true for young people who are looked after.

Going to court or having a court order placed on them can be very distressing for young people. One way of helping a young person to better understand the situation is to give them as much information as possible. This section sets out what many of the legal terms mean. It does not cover criminal law.

Going to court—implications and support for carers

Foster carers play a vital role in helping the courts make the right decisions about the future of the child.

Court visits are an essential part of fostering. There was a time when the foster carer was not involved in the court proceedings. Today, it is recognised that carers, who see the fostered child on a day-to-day basis, have valuable information about the child that social workers and lawyers, who only see the child occasionally, can never have.

For the sake of the child it is vital that foster carers are well prepared for court hearings. So that you can feel more comfortable and better prepared when attending court, the following tips could be useful:

- **Know the legal status:** this means understanding the range of orders that the court can make, or have made, concerning the child. The order will cover such things as 'parental visits', 'curfews' and many more; see the rest of this section for details.
- **Understand the role of the guardian ad litem:** see page 172.
- **Keep records and have them with you in court:** keeping records of such things as placement agreements, reviews, correspondence; even your own hand written observations can be extremely valuable in proving a point or establishing facts in court. A foster carer who is 'organised' will always be viewed in a better light than one who is not.
- **Attend reviews and conferences about the foster child:** you have a right to attend these meetings and at them you will learn what applications and recommendations are to be made to the court, as well as gaining other useful information about the child.
- **Attend any interim or directional hearings:** these are hearings that take place when a court is unable to sit, but where a delay is not in the interest of the child. An interim hearing could occur for example where a local authority is seeking an interim care order following an emergency protection order. Directional hearings set the dates for other hearings.
- **Understand the importance of documentary evidence:** all cases involving children rely heavily on documentary evidence; hence the need for records to be kept. You may be required to write to the court and if so it is wise to seek the help of a legal advisor. Make sure however that you write in your own words, do not let anyone put in jargon or technical language. Using your own words will help you make your point better.
- **Know who will be in court:** in the Magistrates Court there will be three magistrates. There will be a clerk to guide proceedings and take notes. In County and High Courts there will be a person to record what is said but the judge runs the court. There will be an usher to call you in and you will be invited to swear an oath on the bible or to 'affirm' if you do not wish to swear on the bible.
- **Understand the way things are done in court:** before going to court it is a good idea, time permitting, to visit the court to watch a similar hearing to your own. That way you will have a good idea of what to expect. Or, talk to your legal advisor, or read the leaflet *Signposts in Foster Care: Going to Court in England and Wales*, obtainable from NFCA.

Being looked after or being accommodated

There are just two ways a child comes into 'care'.

1. **Being looked after:** this means that a court order has been issued (see following pages for details of the different types of orders). Parental responsibility may be shared between the local authority and the parents. All decisions made about a child should be made in consultation with the child and parents.

2. **Being accommodated:** a child under 16 may only be accommodated with the consent of the parents or those with parental responsibility. It is entirely voluntary and there is no court order. It means that social services provide somewhere for a child to live if:
   - There is no one who has parental responsibility for the child.
   - The child has been lost or abandoned or has been thrown out of home.
   - The person caring for the child cannot provide accommodation or care either temporarily or permanently.
   - The child might suffer ill-treatment from another person.
   - The police or the court have asked social services to provide accommodation for the child.

When the child is ready, explain what being accommodated or being looked after means.

The Children Act 1989; The Children (Scotland) Act 1995 and The Children (Northern Ireland) Order 1995

It may be necessary for the child to go to court if, for example, their parents and social services can't agree on the best plan for their safety and well-being in the future. Court orders are only made when the best interests of the child can be achieved by that order, and when it is better than making no order. In Scotland a Children's Hearing may convene but at present children may not attend.

Carers may need to:
- Explain to the child the reasons for attendance at court.
- Explain the decisions the court could make.
- Prepare the child for going to court.

If there is a court order then it will automatically end when a child is 18 unless it is stopped by the court earlier or the child marries.

There may be a Guardian ad Litem (GAL) (Curator ad Litem or Safeguarder in Scotland) appointed to talk about the child's wishes and feelings. In addition a solicitor will be appointed to represent the child. If the child is of sufficient understanding they may attend the court with the solicitor. Occasionally the GAL will appoint their own solicitor if there is a differing of opinions. Carers should ensure that the child's view is heard. An interpreter may be necessary.

Children are looked after by the local authority if they are either accommodated or a court has made an order committing them to the care of the local authority. If a child is being accommodated by the local authority there is no court order.

The court must:
- Consider what is best for the child including contact with families.
- Make sure that whatever is to happen, happens as soon as possible.
- See that nothing changes unless it is better for the child.

The court must also consider:
- What the child wants and any needs the child may have.
- What the effect will be on the child of any changes.
- The age, sex, background, race, culture, language or anything else that might be appropriate such as brothers and sisters.
- Any problems there may have been in the past or are likely to be in future.
- The ability of the parents, guardians or carers to meet those needs.

On the following pages there is a brief explanation of the various orders that might be imposed.

Court orders: a summary of what they mean

Child Assessment Order

This is made by the court stating that the parents or those with parental responsibility must take the child to the specified place e.g. doctor's, hospital, health centre, so the child may be assessed or someone allowed to examine the child.

It is made:
- where the parents or those responsible have refused to co-operate
- the local authority or authorised person thinks the child might be in danger of significant harm but the child is in no immediate danger

If after looking at all the evidence, immediate action is needed then an Emergency Protection Order will be applied for.

The child may be asked to have a medical examination, either physical or psychiatric, but they may refuse provided they fully understand what is going on.

Emergency Protection Order

This is made if the court has reason to believe that:
- children will come to significant harm if they continue to live where they are or if they are removed from where they are staying
- they are suffering significant harm and their parent carers will not allow doctors or social workers to see them and the harm is likely to continue if they are not removed

The order cannot be stopped or challenged within the first 72 hours. After that it may be challenged in court providing the parent or carer was not present at the initial hearing. It can last up to eight days and then be extended for a further seven days. The child may be asked to have a medical examination, either physical or psychiatric, but may refuse provided they fully understand what is going on. This refusal can be overridden under certain circumstances.

These last two orders may be made at the same time.

Exclusion Order (Scotland only)

It is made to allow the alleged abuser to be removed from the home rather than the child.

Interim Care Order

An Interim Care Order will often follow an Emergency Protection Order. This gives the court time to collect more information and is normally made for not more than eight weeks. Sometimes further ICOs can be made which will last up to four weeks each. There should be as few Interim Care Orders as possible to avoid delay in making a final decision.

The child may be asked to have a medical examination, either physical or psychiatric, but can refuse provided they fully understand.

Usually parents will have contact with their child under Interim Orders.

Care Order

This is made by the court stating that social services must look after the child and provide accommodation. A care order gives social services parental responsibility jointly with the parents. Children should be encouraged to see their families and friends unless the court states otherwise.

It is made if the court thinks the child might be:
- Suffering significant harm or likely to suffer significant harm.
- The care being given is not what a parent should give or the child is beyond the parents' control.
- If making the order will help the child.

It lasts until one of the following happens:
- The young person reaches the age of 18.
- The child is adopted.
- A supervision or residence order is made.
- The court stops the order.
- The child, their parents, social services or the person with parental responsibility asks the court to stop the order and the court agrees.

Contact Order

This is made by the court stating that the person with whom the child lives must allow the child to stay with or visit anyone mentioned in the order. Carers should allow the child to visit, stay with them, write to them or speak on the phone according to the rules agreed by the court.

It is made if any of the following ask for it and the court agrees: the child, the parent or guardian, the foster carers if the child has been living with them for three years or someone close to the child. In fact anyone may apply.

It lasts until the child is 16 or until the court agrees it is no longer necessary. In exceptional circumstances it may last until the young person is 18 if the court thinks it is necessary.

Interim Supervision Order

Sometimes an interim order is made for up to eight weeks so that more information can be collected. Another may be issued for a further four weeks if necessary.

Supervision Order

This is issued when a supervisor, usually from social services, is appointed to advise, help and befriend a child and to make sure any other conditions the court set are carried out.

It is made when social services are worried that the child may be suffering harm or is likely to suffer harm because the care given is not what it should be, or when the child is beyond the parents' control.

It lasts usually for up to a year but no longer than three years and not after the child is 18 years. It can be stopped if a care order is made or if any of the interested parties apply to the court and the court agrees to stop the order.

Residence Order

This is a court order stating with whom the child must live.

It means:
- The child must live with whoever is specified in the order and that person will be given parental responsibility if they haven't got it already.
- The child cannot leave the country for more than a month (nor can the child change their surname) without the written permission of whoever has parental responsibility or the court.
- Any interested party can apply to have it stopped at any time.

It lasts usually until the child is 16 but occasionally until the young person is 18 years old.

Prohibited Steps Order

This is an order made by the court stating that certain things cannot happen without the court's permission. The court won't make a prohibited steps order if better arrangements can be made or if the child is already under a care order.

It lasts until the child is 16 unless there are exceptional reasons for extending it.

Specific Issue Order

This is an order made by the court when there is a disagreement about how the child should be brought up; it might be about schooling, religion, health care, etc. It means the court will decide, after consulting with others, what should be done and how it should be done in the interests of the child. A specific issue order won't be made if there is a better way to sort things out or if there is a care order.

It lasts usually no longer than until the child is 16 years old.

The child's parents or guardians, anyone who has a residence order for the child or the person who applied for the first order to be made, may apply to have it stopped.

Family Assistance Order

This is sometimes made after the child's parents get divorced or a couple separate.

A court welfare officer or someone from social services is appointed to advise, help and befriend the child, their family, the person caring for the child, or the person named on a Contact Order. The person named in the court order must be allowed to visit the child regularly and be told of any change of address.

It lasts for no more than six months unless a new order is made.

Adoption

See also page 33.

There are over half a million adopted people living in Britain today. Young people aged 12–18 are not adopted very often at present. Adoption is usually for the younger child, but sometimes, young people in the 12–18 age group may want to know about adoption.

What is an Adoption Order?

This is a court order: the court decides whether an adoption can go ahead. There may be changes in the Adoption Laws in the future and there are changes taking place in practice in anticipation.

The family the young person lives with may want to adopt them, or the young person may ask their family to adopt them. Sometimes social services will try to find a suitable family who want to adopt the child and suggest it to them.

In all cases the social worker will talk it through with everyone concerned and fill in the necessary forms. Then the family apply to the court and someone will be appointed to look at all the circumstances and information and then make recommendations to the court.

What does being freed for adoption mean?

This means that the young person has been released from their birth parents' responsibility in preparation for being adopted but must be looked after by social services until the adoption is finalised. It also means that they are protected and no one can do anything until the court decides whether or not an adoption can go ahead.

What is an adoption panel?

This is a group of between five and ten people, including someone from social services, teachers, health visitors, someone from the adoption agency or adoptive parents, who meet to make sure:

- the adoption is in the young person's best interests
- the family is suitable to adopt
- the young person is suitable for that family

Independent Visitor

An Independent Visitor may be appointed if it is:

- thought necessary when the first plan is drawn up
- decided at a review
- the child agrees

Sometimes a child may have a seperate advocate or a mentor to help them. They do much the same things with the child as an Independent Visitor and will be trained for the work. However, they are normally volunteers.

Why does a child need an Independent Visitor?

A child may benefit from someone else coming to visit them if they are not in contact with or hardly ever see their parents. However, if the child is in a settled home or foster home and has lots of other friends and visitors it may not be thought necessary.

If it is not possible for a child to live in a placement with carers of similar background, race or culture then an Independent Visitor could become a link with a child's own community.

What will Independent Visitors do?

- They will try to help by advising, befriending or supporting the child.
- They will try to help a child in their social, emotional, religious or cultural development.
- They may advise a child on any matter they think fit or if the child asks for help.
- In some situations they may act as an advocate, say where the child feels they are not being cared for properly or their views are not being listened to or considered.

What type of person is an Independent Visitor?

- Someone who can relate to children.
- Someone who has their well-being at heart.
- The Independent Visitor may be only, say, 25 years old or much older, say the child's grandparent's age.
- They will be a good listener and will be specially chosen to work with children.

How do I get an Independent Visitor?

Normally the child's social worker will have details of the procedure. If carers think that the child would benefit from having someone to take an interest in them outside the foster carer's home they should discuss this with the child and also find out the relevant procedures.

What happens if the child doesn't like the person chosen?

There will be several getting-to-know-you meetings where both the child and the visitor can decide whether to go ahead with the arrangement or not. At all times the child's best interest and wishes come first.

How long will Independent Visitors keep visiting?

- It may be only for a short while until relationships with parents improve or it may go on for several years. It all depends on the circumstances.
- It will be discussed at every review.

Will they always visit the child?

No, sometimes they will, or the child may go out and meet them 'on neutral ground', or go on a visit. Occasionally the Independent Visitor may also invite the child to the Visitor's own home. This may, of course, be subject to certain controls.

Are Independent Representatives the same?

An Independent Representative (or IR or independent rep) is not the same. An IR is a person who visits children who are in secure accommodation to ensure the children are treated fairly and receive suitable care. They are independent both of the secure unit and of the care authority.

They visit every child as soon as possible after admission and at regular intervals afterwards. They will listen to the child, tell them of their rights, take up matters on behalf of the child and help them write letters or see the appropriate person.

Guardian ad Litem (GAL) (Curator ad Litem (CAL) or Safeguarder)

In Scotland when an application for adoption is made a Curator ad Litem may be appointed. Adoption cases may be heard in the Court of Session or more usually in the local Sheriff Court. At other times where a child's case comes before a children's hearing, a Safeguarder may be appointed. Much of the work of these two groups are similar to the role of the GAL.

What is Guardian ad Litem (Curator ad Litem or Safeguarder)?

Ad Litem is Latin and means dealing with the law, so Guardian ad Litem is a person who looks after a child's interests if someone has applied for a court order. A GAL is appointed by the court, and does not work for social services.

What do these people do?

- Listen to what a child wants now and in the future.
- Talk to the child, the parents, grandparents and anyone else who is important to the child.
- Talk to teachers, social workers, health visitors and anyone else who can give advice or help.
- Read reports about the child and their family.
- Work out what is best for the child.

The guardian will chose a suitable solicitor who will be able to explain to the court what is best for the child.

Who becomes a Guardian ad Litem, Curator ad Litem or Safeguarder?

Every local authority must have a panel of people who can give independent advice and reports to the court. Social services can ask people to go on the panel or people can apply themselves. Either way they are interviewed and have to show that they are suitable for the job. They must represent the child's view.

After listening to and thinking about what everyone has said, the GAL will write a report about the child. The report will give advice on what the guardian thinks is best for the child. The guardian will always write down how the child feels about the plans and what the child wishes to happen.

After the final hearing the guardian should meet the child to explain what has been decided.

Guardianship

What is a guardian?

A guardian is a person who is given full parental responsibility for a child because the parents have died. The guardian will have the same responsibilities that their parents would have had.

Who can appoint a guardian?

- anyone with parental responsibility (p 174)
- any other guardian
- a court

When does guardianship stop?

- when the child is 18
- when the court orders it to stop
- when either the child or someone with parental responsibility applies to the court to have it stopped and the court agrees it is in the interest of the child.

Wardship and the Inherent Jurisdiction

Wardship gives the court continuing responsibility for the child. The Children Acts have reduced the use of Wardship with the introduction of Prohibited Steps Orders, Specific Issues Orders and Residence Orders which have largely taken its place. Wardship cannot be used when there is a Care Order.

Occasionally the court will use the Inherent Jurisdiction in order to protect a child. What this means is that the court has retained certain powers to enable it to take action if the need arises and it is in the best interest of the child. Local authorities can only use the Inherent Jurisdiction order in exceptional circumstances, when other laws do not enable the child to be protected from significant harm.

Parental responsibility

By law there are certain things parents should and should not do when bringing up a child. They must ensure that a child gets correct medical treatment, full education, and that physical, moral and religious needs are met.

Who has parental responsibility?

If a child's father and mother were married to each other when the child was born, or have since married, they both automatically have parental responsibility. Parents only lose parental responsibility if the child gets adopted.

If the court makes a care order the local authority acquires joint 'parental responsibility' along with the parents. If there is a dispute then the local authority view is taken.

Foster or residential carers do not have parental responsibility but may have some day-to-day parental responsibility delegated to them by the parents or by the local authority.

What if my parents didn't get married?

Only the mother has parental responsibility automatically. If the father was not married to the mother he can:
- Apply to the court for parental responsibility.
- Draw up a formal agreement with the mother which must be registered with the court.
- Ask to be made the child's guardian.
- Be granted a residence order by the court.

Natural fathers will not automatically get parental responsibility although this is likely to change in the future.

Who else can get parental responsibility?

- Parents can delegate it to someone else, but they won't lose it themselves.
- An adoptive parent automatically gets parental responsibility.
- A guardian.
- The person with whom the child is living if a residence order is made.
- The local authority gets it if a care order or emergency protection order is made.

How long does parental responsibility last?

Until a person is 18 (16 in Scotland), but a court order may cancel it before then.

Changing names

Many children want to be called by a different name for many reasons such as:

- Bad memories of their father or mother or of their step father or mother.
- To try to create a new identity.
- Because it's easier to be known by the name of the rest of the family: this often happens when children are fostered.
- Just because they simply don't like the name they've got.

Can children change their names?

Children can change their names by simply asking people to call them by any name they wish.

They cannot change their name for legal purposes without permission from whoever has parental responsibility for them. Names may be changed by deed poll or statutory declaration. This proves to others that the child has changed names. Documents must be drawn up by a solicitor. There will be a charge for this work, and someone should find out what it is before instructing the solicitor to proceed.

What happens if a child is on a care order or residence order?

Children can ask people to call them any first name they wish at any time, but to change their surname they must have the written permission of whoever has parental responsibility for them, or the court. In general, carers should encourage children to keep their own names.

Why should anyone bother to go to court to change a name?

As we said earlier there is nothing to stop anyone changing their name but if children decide that the change is permanent then it is better to do it formally. If they don't it may cause problems later in life, for example, if they want to join the armed forces.

Section 10: Other Information

Useful names and addresses

Many of these organisations offer good value, informative material.

National Foster Care Association (NFCA)
87 Blackfriars Road
London SE1 8HA

Tel: 020 7620 6400
Fax: 020 7620 6401
e-mail: nfca@fostercare.org.uk

The National Foster Care Association (NFCA) aims to ensure the highest standards of care for all children and young people who are fostered, through the provision of training, advice, support, information and consultancy services. Founded in 1974, NFCA works to: define high standards and best practice for foster care; assist local authorities, agencies and individuals to work effectively in the best interests of fostered children; inform, influence and persuade policy makers on foster care issues; and improve public understanding of foster care.

British Agencies for Adoption and Fostering (BAAF)
Skyline House
200 Union Street
London, SE1 OLY

Tel: 020 7593 2000

BAAF promotes public understanding of adoption and fostering; develops high standards of practice amongst child care and other professionals; provides high quality training tailored to meet specific needs; acts as an independent voice in the field of child care to inform and influence policy-makers

National Children's Bureau (NCB)
8 Wakley Street
London ECV 70E

Tel: 020 7275 9441

National Children's Bureau works to identify and promote the well-being and interests of all children and young people across every aspect of their lives. NCB encourages professionals and policy makers to see the needs of the whole child and emphasises the importance of multi-disciplinary, cross-agency partnerships. NCB undertakes high quality research, promotes good practice, and ensures that the views of children and young people are taken into account.

NCB houses the Children's Residential Care Unit and undertakes research and practice development to develop effective services for children in public care.

For more information about NCB's vast range of publications, information resources, conferences, training, and consultancy work, please call the marketing unit on 020 7843 6047.

Voice for the Child in Care
Unit 4 Pride Court
80-82 White Lion Street
London N1 5PF

Tel: 020 7833 5792
Fax: 020 7833 8637
Freephone for children: 0808 800 5792

Voice for the Child in Care provides advocacy services for children and young people looked after, including specialist visiting services to children's homes and for fostering agencies. This is supported by a legal adviser and freephone for children and young people in care.

VCC also provide an advocacy service for runaways: *YRU Running*.

VCC has a network of volunteer visitors to secure units throughout the country, runs independent person services for complaints and secure review panels, provides training, consultation and publications including a book for young people in care—*Shout to be Heard*.

The Who Cares? Trust	Tel: 020 7251 3117
Kemp House	Fax: 020 7251 3123,
152–160 City Road	E-mail: mallbox@thewhocarestrust.org.uk
London EC1V 2NP	Website: http://www.thewhocarestrust.org.uk

The Who Cares? Trust aims to help raise the profile of young people living in care in the 21st Century. It offers children and young people in public care the chance to have their say through the Who Cares? Linkline Freecall 0500 564570: offering confidential support and information.

The nationally acclaimed Who Cares? magazine for today's teenager in care is recommended by the Association of Directors of Social Services programmes in Health, Education, Disability, Lifeskills and Preparation for Employment.

Organisations with specific concerns

Abuse

Childline
Freepost 1111
London N1 OBR
Freephone: 0800 1111

Kidscape
2 Grosvenor Gardens
London SW1W ODH
Tel: 020 7730 3300

Adoption

Post Adoption Centre
5 Torriano Mews
Torriano Avenue
London NW5 2RZ
Tel: 020 7284 0555

National Children's Homes
85 Highbury Park
London N5 1UD
Tel: 020 7226 2033

National Organisation for Counselling
Adoptees and their Parents (NORCAP)
3 New Street
Headington
Oxford OX3 7AJ
Tel: 01865 750554

British Agencies for Adoption
and Fostering (BAAF)
Skyline House
200 Union Street
London SE1 OLY
Tel: 020 7593 2000

AIDS/HIV

AIDS Information Service will send leaflets
Tel: 0800 555777

Bereavement

Cruse Bereavement Care
Cruse House
126 Sheen Road
Richmond
Surrey TW9 1UR
Tel: 020 8940 4818
Helpline: 081 332 7117

Care

Advocacy Service for Children (ASC)
Black in Care
Elin House
86 Bellender Road
London SE15 4RG
Freephone: 0800 616101

National Society for the Prevention of
Cruelty to Children (NSPCC)
42 Curtain Road
London EC2A 3NH
Tel: 020 7825 2500

National Foster Care Association (NFCA)
87 Blackfriars Road
London SE1 8HA
020 7620 6400
Helpline: 020 7620 2100

Depression

The Samaritans
10 The Grove
Slough SL1 1QP
Tel: 01753 532713

Discrimination and racism

Black Issues Project (BAAF)
Skyline House
200 Union Street
London SE1 OLX
Tel: 020 7593 2000

Institute of Race Relations
2–6 Leeke Street
London WC1X 9HS
Tel: 020 7837 0041

The Equal Opportunities Commission
Overseas House
Quay Street
Manchester M3 3HN
Tel: 0161 833 9244

The Commission for Racial Equality
Elliot House
10—12 Allington Street
London SW1E 5EH
Tel: 020 7828 7022
Birmingham: 0121 632 4544
Manchester: 0161 831 7782
Leicester: 01533 517 852
Leeds: 01532 434 413
Edinburgh: 0131 226 5186

Disability

The Royal National Institute for
Deaf People
105 Gower Street
London WC1E 6AH
Tel: 020 7387 8033

The National Autistic Society
393 City Road
London EC1 1NG
Tel: 020 7833 2299
Fax: 020 7833 9666

British Epilepsy Association
Gate Way Drive
Yeadon
Leeds LS19 7XY
Tel: 0113 210 8800
Freephone: 0808 800 5050

British Deaf Association
1–3 Worship Street
London, EC2A 2AB
Tel: 020 7588 3520

Royal Association for Disability and
Rehabilitation (RADAR)
Unit 12, 250 City Road
London EC1V 8AF
Tel: 020 7250 3222

Disabled Living Foundation
380–384 Harrow Road
London W9 2HU
Tel: 020 7289 6111

Riding for the Disabled
Avenue R
National Agricultural Centre
Kenilworth
Warwickshire CV8 2LY
Tel: 02476 696510

Guide Dogs for the Blind
Hillfields
Burghfield
Reading RG7 3YG
Tel: 01734 835555

Spinal Injuries Association
Newpoint House
76 St. James Lane
London N10 3DF
Counselling: 020 8883 4296 (Direct line)
General enquiries: 020 8444 2121

Association for Spina Bifida and
Hydrocephalus (ASBAH)
ASBAH House
42 Park Road
Peterborough
PE1 2UQ

British Sports Association for the Disabled
Solecast House
13–27 Brunswick Place
London N1 6DX
Tel: 020 7490 4919

Royal National Institute for the Blind
224 Gt. Portland Street
London W1N 6AA
Tel: 020 73881266

SCOPE (Spastics Society)
6 Market Road
London N7 9PW
Tel: 020 7619 7100

MENCAP
123 Golden Lane
London EC1Y 0RT
Tel: 020 7454 0454

Drug abuse

Release (Legal and Drugs Advice)
388 Old Street
London EC1V 9LT
Emergency Tel: 020 7603 8654
(24-hour emergency telephone service)

Eating

Eating Disorders Association
1st Floor Wensum House
103 Prince of Wales Road
Norwich NR1 1DW
Tel: 01603 619090

Eating Disoder Team
Department of Psychological Medicine
The Hospital for Sick Children
Great Ormond Street
London WC1N 3JN
Tel: 020 7829 8679

Child & Adolescent Eating
Disorder Service
Harewood House
Springfield Hospital
Glenburnie Road
London SW17 7DJ
Tel: 020 8682 6747

Vegetarian Society
Parkdale
Dunham Road
Altrincham
Cheshire WA14 4QG
Tel: 0161 928 0793

Health

British Heart Foundation
14 Fitzharding Street
London W1H 4DH
Tel: 020 7935 0185

Health Education Authority
Hamilton House
Mabledon Place
London WC1H 9TX
Tel: 020 7383 3833

Law

Children's Legal Centre
20 Compton Terrace
London N1 2UN
Tel: 020 7359 6251

Listening

The Samaritans
10 The Grove
Slough SL1 1QP
Tel: 0753 532713
       020 7284 4793

Ombudsmen

Greater London, Kent, Surrey, East
Anglia and most of Central England
Mr E.B.C. Osmotherleyey
Local Government Ombudsman
21 Queen Anne's Gate
London SW1H 9BU
Tel: 020 7915 3210

The East Midlands and the
North of England
Mrs Patricia Thomas
Local Government Ombudsman
Beverley House
17 Shipton Road
York YO30 5FZ
Tel: 01904 663200

The South West, the West, the South, East and
West Sussex
Mr Gerry White
Local Government Ombudsman
The Oaks
Westwood Way
Westwood Business Park
Coventry CV4 8JB
Tel: 01476 695999

Safety

Child Accident Prevention Trust
18–10 Farringdon Lane
London EC1R 3AU
Tel: 020 7608 3828

Your local fire station

Department of Trade and Industry
DTI Publications in Print
Tel: 020 7510 0174

Home safety officer in the Department of
Environmental Health in your local authority

Sex and sexuality

Brook Advisory Centres
153a East Street
London SE17 2SD
Helpline: 020 7708 1234

Lesbian and Gay Switchboard
Tel: 020 7837 7324

Family Planning Association
27–35 Mortimer Street
London W1N 7RJ
Tel: 020 7837 4044

Solvent abuse

Re-Solv
30 High Street
Stone
Staffordshire ST15 8AW
Tel: 01785 817885

Training

National Foster Care Association (NFCA)
87 Blackfriers Road
London SE1 BHA
Tel: 020 7620 6400

British Agencies for Adoption and
Fostering (BAAF)
Skyline House
200 Union Street
London SE1 OLY
Tel: 020 7593 2000

Bibliography and References

Ahmad, W.U. (Ed.) (1993). *Race and Health in Contemporary Britain*. Open University.

Aldgate, J., and Simmonds, J. (Eds.) (1988). *Direct Work with Children*. Batsford: BAAF.

Althea, (1981). *When Uncle Bob Died*. Dinosaur.

Althea, (1989). *I Have Cancer*. Dinosaur.

BAAF (1987–1990). *Range of Workbooks for Use with Children and Young People*. BAAF.

BAAF (1991). *Children who Foster*, Training materials. BAAF.

BAAF (1998). Carer Held Health Record. BAAF.

Barn, R. (1993). *Black Children in the Public Care System*. Batsford: BAAF.

Batty, D. (1993). *HIV Infection and Children in Need*. BAAF.

Batty, D., and Bayley, N. (1984). *In Touch with Children*, Training pack. BAAF.

Bower, S., and Bower, G.H. (1991). *Asserting Yourself, A Practical Guide for the Positive Change*. Addison & Wesley.

British Red Cross (2000). *First Aid for Children Fast: For Parents and Carers*. Dorling Kindersley.

Buchanan, A., Wheal, A., Walker, D., Macdonald, S., and Coker, R. (1993). *Answering Back, Report by Young People Being Looked After Under the Children Act 1989*. Department of Social Work Studies.

Bullock, R., Little, M., and Millham, S. (1993). *Going Home, The Return of Children Separated from their Families*. Dartmouth.

Burningham, J. (1984). *Grandpa*. Cape.

Collins, D., Tank, M., and Basith, A. (1993). *Concise Guides to Customs of Minority Ethnic Religions*. Arena.

Couldrick, A. (1991). *When Your Mum or Dad Has Cancer*. Sobell.

Damani, P., Churcher, P., Birch, J., Khaira, A., and Warren, V. *Play with Confidence: A Training Pack for Those Wishing to Introduce Children to Multiracial Britain*.

Daws, D. (1993). *Through the Night, Helping Parents and Sleeping Infants*. Free Association Books.

Department for Education (1994). *Special Educational Needs, A Guide for Parents*. DFE.

Department of Health (1989). *The Care of Children; Principles and Practice*. HMSO.

Department of Health (1990). *An Introduction to the Children Act*. HMSO.

Department of Health (1993). *Looking After Children, Assessment and Action Records*. HMSO.

Department of Health, (1990). *Protecting Children: A Guide for Social Workers Undertaking a Comprehensive Assessment*. HMSO.

Department of Health, (1991). *Patterns and Outcomes in Care in Child Placement*. HMSO.

Department of Health, (1991). *The Children Act 1989—Range of Leaflets and Guides for Parents and Young People*. HMSO.

Department of Health, (1991). *The Children Act 1989, Guidance and Regulations, Volumes 1–9*. HMSO.

Department of Health, (1991). *The Children Act 1989, Guidance and Regulations, Index*. HMSO.

Department of Health, (1991). *Working Together Under the Children Act 1989, A Guide to Arrangements for Inter-agency Co-operation for The Protection of Children from Abuse*. HMSO.

Duckley, D., Orritt, B., and Thelwell, D. (1990). *Going into Care*. The Children's Society.

Family Rights Group (1991). *The Children Act 1989, Working in Partnership with Families*. HMSO.

Gambe, D., Gomes, J., Kapur, V., Rangel, M., and Stubbs, P. (1992). *Improving Practice with Children and Families*. CCETSW.

Hampshire County Council (1991). *My Guidebook*. Ashford Open Learning.

Heegaard, M. (1991). *When Someone Has a Very Serious Illness*. Woodland.

Heegaard, M. (1991). *When Someone Very Special Dies*. Woodland.

HMSO, (1989). *Access to Personal Files (Social Services), Regulations*. HMSO.

HMSO, (1989). *The Children Act*. HMSO.

Jeynes, L. (1993). *Would you be a Foster Carer?* Linda Jeynes.

Karmi, G. (Ed.). *The Ethnic Health Fact File*. The Health and Ethnicity Programme.

Lindon, J. (1993). *Child Development from Birth to Eight: A Practical Focus*. National Children's Bureau.

McCartt, Hess, P., and Ohman Proch, K. (1993). *Contact: Managing Visits to Children Looked After Away from Home*. BAAF.

Millham, S., Bullock, R., Hosie, K., and Little, M. (1986). *Lost in Care. The Problem of Maintaining Links Between Children in Care and Their Families.* Gower.

MNDA. *When Someone Special Has Motor Neurone Disease.* MNDA.

National Foster Care Association (1999). *Report and Recommendations of the UK Joint Working Party on Foster Care.* NFCA.

National Foster Care Association (1999). *UK National Standards for Foster Care.* NFCA.

National Foster Care Association (1999). *Code of Practice on the recruitment, assessment, approval, training, management and support of foster carers.* NFCA.

National Foster Care Association. A range of leaflets on many areas of foster care. NFCA.

Neuberger, J. (1987). *Caring for Dying People of Different Faiths.* Lisa Sainsbury.

Newell, P. (1991). *The UN Convention and Children's Rights in the UK.* National Children's Bureau.

NSPCC. *Protect Your Child: A Guide about Child Abuse for Parents.* NSPCC.

Parents Aid (1991). *A Guide for Families: Your Child and Social Services.* Parents Aid.

PHAB. *Teachers' Notes on Physical Disability,* Hampshire Project. PHAB.

Porteous, M.A. (1985). *Porteous Problem Checklist and Inventory of Adolescent Problems.* NFER-Nelson.

Ryan, A., and Walker, R. (1999). *Life Story Work.* BAAF.

Schulz, C.M. (1990). *Why, Charlie Brown, Why?* Ravette.

Sheridan, M. *Good Enough Parenting.* Adcock & White.

Simmonds, P. (1981). *Fred.* Puffin.

Stickney, D. (1990). *Waterbugs and Dragonflies.* Mowbray.

Swarup, N. *Equal Voice, Report no 22.* Social Services Research and Information Unit, Portsmouth Polytechnic.

Thomson, R. (Ed.) (1993). *Religion, Ethnicity Sex Education: Exploring the Issues.* Sex Education Forum, National Children's Bureau.

Triselioti, J., and Marsh, P. (1993). *Prevention and Re-unification.* Batsford: BAAF.

United Nations (1989). *The Convention on the Rights of the Child.* UNICEF.

Varley, S. (1985). *Badger's Parting Gifts.* Collins.

Wessex Regional Health Authority (1992). *Eat Well, Be Well.* Wessex Regional Health Authority.

West, S. (1993). *Open Sez Me, The Magic of Pleasant Discoveries.* Spring, Summer, Autumn, Winter.

Wheal, A. with Buchanan, A. (1999). *Answers, You and the Young people in Your Care.* Pavilion Publishing

Loose leaf version

We have found that many organisations want to provide their carers with the basic information contained in this book while simultaneously giving details of their own local information, procedures and forms.

To help with this, we can supply this book as loose leaf sets which you can incorporate with your own materials in your own folders (minimum order 25 sets).

We can offer substantial discounts on bulk purchases of either the book itself or loose leaf sets.

For example, at publication date, 100 loose leaf sets would cost less than £14 per copy, or you could get 500 for less than £10 each!

Please contact us for an up to date quote or to discuss your particular needs: *we're here to help*.

Tel: 01297 443948   Fax: 01297 442722
e-mail: help@russellhouse.co.uk

Russell House Publishing
4, St. George's House
Uplyme Road
Lyme Regis DT7 3LS